MACROECONOMIC ISSUES TODAY

W9-CHB-388

Alternative Approaches
Fourth Edition

MACROECONOMIC ISSUES TODAY

Alternative Approaches
Fourth Edition

Robert B. Carson
State University College, Oneonta, New York

St. Martin's Press
New York

This book is dedicated to my mother,
Catherine Postlewaite Carson

Library of Congress Catalog Card Number: 86-60649
Copyright © 1987 by St. Martin's Press, Inc.
All Rights Reserved.
10987
fedcba
For information, write St. Martin's Press, Inc.
175 Fifth Avenue, New York, N.Y. 10010

cover design: Ben Santora

ISBN: 0-312-50340-7

ACKNOWLEDGMENTS

From E.Y. Harburg and Jay Gorney, "Brother Can You Spare a Dime?" Lyrics by E.Y. Harburg. Music by Jay Gorney. © 1932 by Warner Bros., Inc. Copyright renewed. All rights reserved. Used by permission.

Fig. 6–1 from Michael I. Boskin, ed., *The Crisis in Social Security.* San Francisco: Institute for Contemporary Studies, 1977, p. 8. Reprinted by permission.

Preface

Since the first appearance of *Macroeconomic Issues Today*, and its companion volume, *Microeconomic Issues Today*, in 1980, the author has tried to select topical issues that get to the heart of varieties of economic reasoning and deal with interesting and current economic problems. This, the fourth edition, is no exception. Instructors who have used earlier versions will note very considerable changes in the updating of the book; little in economics has stood still over the past ten years. I have benefited in this as in past revision efforts from correspondence from dozens of instructors and students who have taken time to suggest changes or simply comment on the book's content.

Among the changes longtime users of the book will notice are (1) a strengthening of the presentation of both the Conservative and Radical paradigms in the introduction and a certain "modernizing" of the Radical argument throughout the text, (2) a stronger and more up-to-date debate on fiscal policy alternatives, (3) a new issue on government deficits, and (4) a virtual rewriting of the old international trade issue to face the new trade and finance realities of the late 1980s. Of course, throughout the book I have inserted the most recent available references and data and added new tables and figures so that all the information is as fresh as it can possibly be. All in all, *Macroeconomic Issues Today* has undergone in this revision the most extensive rewriting and reorganizing since its original publication.

All these changes are designed to enhance, not alter, the pedagogical approach followed in earlier editions. As before, the book requires no background in the methods of economic analysis, and as much as possible it avoids the use of economic jargon in favor of everyday language. This edition of *Macroeconomic Issues Today*, like earlier ones, stresses the ideological choices that exist in economic thought and that often cause ordinary citizens to be confused about what economists *do* and what economists *believe*. As ever, it is meant to be a provocative book, more interested in provoking discussion and thought than in presenting "right" solutions to problems. It remains committed to the belief that real economic solutions are possible in a democratic society only when all alternatives are known and considered.

Let me explain why I undertook this project in the first place. All too frequently, students begin their study of economics with the impression that economists are bland and monolithic when discussing important issues confronting the general society. We may as well admit that the profession sometimes exhibits a tendency to blandness in its public utterances, but surely any supposed unanimity toward social policy questions has vanished. With the rise of an influential radical caucus within the discipline, beginning in the late 1960s, and the more recent resurgence of variations of laissez-faire ideology, any facade of consensus has clearly been broken down. The application of economic theory to issues of public policy more and more reflects a range of choice from Conservative to Liberal to Radical.

For the student struggling with basic theory and analytic tools, as well as for the ordinary citizen overwhelmed by economic data in the newspapers and on the TV evening news, it is hard to avoid confusion over what economists really think about the problems facing the nation. This book begins with the assumption that the answers economists give to policy questions can be usefully compared and analyzed according to the particular biases of their arguments and the probable outcomes of their proposals. In other words, differences in economic logic and interpretation of evidence are not so much a function of skill mastery as they are the expression of strongly held social and political opinions. The book also assumes that economics as a body of knowledge takes on greater meaning and is more readily comprehended when it is viewed in this way.

For each issue, a Conservative, Liberal, and Radical analysis and proposed solution are presented in turn as the valid approach to the problem. On one page, there may be a vigorous and unyielding defense of laissez-faire and the market economy, on another, a program for the elimination or modification of the free market. This is not the way economic analysis and theory are usually taught, but it is what the practice of economics is about. In the real world, the citizen and the economist make public policy choices that protect, attack, or modify the market mechanism. We may defend our positions in terms of economic logic, but behind our proofs lies our political and ideological view of the world. This book attempts to examine the relationship between ideological values and the economic theories and policies that are their outcome.

Since the book presents a wide range of views on a number of currently sensitive issues, it should provoke disagreement, controversy, and discussion. In itself, the book does not urge a particular ideological position or a particular variety of economic analysis. The decision to select or reject this or that point of view is left, as it should be, to the reader.

Each chapter is self-contained and may be assigned in any order the instructor chooses. (The Instructor's Manual provides a grid correlating the chapters here with the chapters in leading principles textbooks.) There are relatively few footnotes or direct references to particular economists, although the ideas of many contemporary economists and schools of economic thought will be apparent. The bibliography at the end is offered for anyone wishing to dig a little deeper into an issue or a particular economic perspective or approach.

The decision to minimize the explicit discussion of technical terms and specific economic concepts in the discussion of contemporary policy issues does not mean the author rejects the importance of formal economic analysis. For instructors using *Macroeconomic Issues Today* along with a conventional principles of economics text, the Instructor's Manual supplies an outline of the pertinent economic concepts. Even instructors using this book as collateral reading may find the manual quite useful.

The basic outline of this book grew out of discussions with Irving Rockwood and my own earlier experience with editing two collections of readings in economics. As the work developed, I received further encouragement in very early stages from Tony Dick and Murray Curtin and at a later and most critical juncture from Bertrand Lummus.

The publication of this new edition has incurred its own special debts, which deserve acknowledgment. Larry Swanson of St. Martin's Press took over the editorial responsibilities for this version and was a steady and encouraging influence in developing a revised and fresh edition. Emily Berleth again served brilliantly as project editor. Professor Jack Adams of the University of Arkansas at Little Rock, Professor James Hanson of Willamette University, and Edward

Salmonsen of Monterey Peninsula College read the manuscript and made many useful suggestions. Denise M. Sheehan of the State University of New York at Albany aided in preparing the Instructor's Manual. And, as always, there were the inspiration and encouragement given by my students, questioning and demanding answers to the "great" economic problems of the day regardless of whether the author had any notion of what the "answer" might be.

Contents

MACROECONOMIC ISSUES TODAY

Alternative Approaches
Fourth Edition

PART 1

INTRODUCTION

Alternative Economic Philosophies

A Survey of Conservative, Liberal, and Radical Critiques

> The ideas of economists, both when they are right and when they are wrong, are more powerful than is commonly understood. Indeed, the world is ruled by little else. Practical men, who believe themselves to be quite exempt from any intellectual influences, are usually the slaves of some defunct economist. Madmen in authority, who hear voices in the air, are distilling their frenzy from some academic scribbler of a few years back.
>
> *John Maynard Keynes, 1936*

Why Do Economists Disagree?

The public appetite for information on economic matters has never been greater. Subscriptions to and reading of a wide variety of business, financial, and general economic publications is a matter of habit with a growing number of Americans. Even ordinary citizens' attention usually heightens as the evening TV news presents its "Business Briefs" and "Economy Watch" segments. Meanwhile, almost a quarter of all American college students have selected business-, management- or economics-related fields as their undergraduate major. However, there is, to many Americans, an annoying irony about the increased interest in economic topics. Although general public literacy in economics has increased exponentially over the past couple of decades, the sharpness of disagreement among economists and the competition among alternative economic explanations have increased just as swiftly.

Paraphrasing George Bernard Shaw, an exasperated President Kennedy, then soliciting economic advice on ways to stimulate a sluggish economy, lamented, "If you laid all economists head to feet, all you would reach is confusion." It is doubtless a view shared by many contemporary evening news watchers. However, the president missed the point. Really what you would reach wouldn't be confusion, it would be different points of view (economists will assure the uninitiated that there is a difference between "confusion" and "different points of view"). Economists, as a group, have rarely been noted for their single-mindedness. Indeed, as one wag noted, if they were, they and their work would not enjoy much attention. Nothing, after all, is quite as dull an area of intellectual activity as one in which everyone agrees with everyone else.

Were it not for the gravity of the subject matter and the fact that so much depends on "being right" in economic affairs, it might be sufficient to account for diversity and disagreement in economic matters as a simple matter of human perversity. Alas, we are compelled to dig a bit deeper in searching for an explanation.

Essentially there are two reasons for economists' holding contrary points of view on matters of economic theory and policy. First of all, there is the possibility that while there may be fundamental agreement on economic values and perspectives and on methods of studying specific data, men and women of essentially the same views and training may still honestly differ in interpretation of the data. Such was the case in the winter of 1984–1985, when "economist bashing" briefly became a popular indoor sport of the Reagan administration. In this case, many economists outside the administration who had previously been enthusiastic supporters of most of the president's programs took a more pessimistic view of the economy's expected future performance than did the president. Some began to talk openly about an impending recession. As recession failed to materialize in early 1985, Reagan supporters, including a number of administration economists, gleefully poked fun at certain other economists whose sophisticated models seemed decidedly less accurate than Ronald Reagan's hunches.*

Although this first type of disagreement within the economics fraternity, and sometimes between economists and political leaders, is "good front-page news" and may actually have significant consequences, it is not nearly as important as the kind of disagreement which reflects different fundamental ethical and political perspectives. In our second instance, disagreement begins with the very way in which economic facts and data are gathered, perceived, and measured and therefore carries through to very different expectations about the outcome of particular economic policies.

The second category of "professional disagreement" is by far the more perplexing—to economists as well as to the general public. Within the profession, there is a strong tendency to avoid discussion of this more basic reason for disagreement among economists. The best-selling introductory economics textbook tries to bury the question this way:

> A reasonable summary of the state of disagreement in economics today would be: Economists are quite divided on central issues of macroeconomics, particularly the role of money. A substantial amount of

---

*Reagan in fact toyed with abolishing the President's Council of Economic Advisors—composed entirely of his own appointees—on the grounds that considering the kind of advice he had been getting, it would be a useful reduction in governmental expenditures. The president might have been better served by taking a longer view on the value of having consensus among economists irrespective of their immediate predictive accuracy. Consensus had not helped Hoover much in 1929 when few conventional economists saw any weakness in the bull market, nor had the consensus on the CEA of Johnson and Nixon in the 1960s prepared the nation for the stagflation of the 1970s.

accord is seen in the microeconomic theory of prices and markets. But on the broad political and ethical issues of economics, economists are as divided as their parents or cousins.*

While such a disclaimer may serve its immediate purpose—to simply get on with the conventional theoretical "stuff" of introductory economics by shoving economic values into the realm of personal politics—it is an evasion not unnoticed by the sharp-eyed student as well as many ordinary people seeking hard answers to hard economic questions. The necessity for making so-called personal value judgments always keeps sneaking into real-world economic discussions: What is the solution to the farm problem? Does the federal deficit really matter? Who should pay how much in taxes? And so on. The fact is that economists not only offer opinions but construct programs dealing with these questions, and they do it as economists, not as "parents and cousins" of economists. Meanwhile, it is perfectly evident that politicians, the "madmen in authority," as John Maynard Keynes described them, are indeed listening to the advice of these "academic scribblers."

The frequent squabbling among economists over desired policy objectives can scarcely be hidden from the public, and such disagreement can be downright unsettling. It often comes as a rude surprise to the person on the street, who, although paying due professional respect to the economists, still sees the economist as a kind of mechanic. When one's car does not start, the car owner expects (at least hopes) that the diagnosis of mechanical trouble given at one garage is exactly the same as what will be heard at any other. If there is one mechanical problem, there should be one mechanical solution. The moral of this comparison is that economics is more than studying a repair manual, and economists are not mechanics.

---

*Paul A. Samuelson and William D. Nordhaus, *Economics*, 12th ed. (New York: McGraw-Hill, 1985), p. 7. The traditional technique has been to divide economics as a science into two parts: *positive economics*, which deals purely with factual relationships such as the level of national output, unemployment, prices, and so on, and *normative economics*, which interprets these facts into goals, which merely reflect individual value judgments. The trouble is, as most economists admit, that these distinctions have blurred. For instance, is the decision not to count those who have "given up" looking for jobs as part of the unemployed a *positive* or *normative* judgment? Indeed, there are few purely factual relationships that don't require some amount of value judgment.

The Role of Ideology

How is such disagreement possible? Isn't economics a science? Economists' answers to that question vary. A common and reasonable enough response is simply that scientists disagree too. While there is much truth to such an answer, it really begs the question. Plainly, the "dismal science" of economics is not a science like physics. While economists may sometimes talk about the laws of supply and demand as if they were eternal verities like the law of gravity, there is abundant anthropological and historical evidence that many societies have behaved quite contrary to the laws of supply and demand. Outside of science fiction, however, there is no denying the law of gravity.

To be sure, economists employ (or at least should employ) the rigor of scientific method and quantitative techniques in collecting data, testing hypotheses, and offering reasonable conclusions and predictions. However, economists deal with different "stuff" from that of their colleagues in the exact sciences. Their data involve human beings and their laboratory is a world of behavior and perception that varies with time and place. On top of this, economists, like all social scientists, are called upon to answer a question not asked of those in the "pure" sciences: "What *ought* to be?" Astronomers, for instance, are not asked what *ought* to be the gravitational relationships of our universe. That would be a nonsense question. Economists, however, cannot evade making some determinations about optimal prices, optimal income distribution, and so forth. Their decisions, while perhaps based upon a genuine effort at neutrality, detachment, and honest evaluation of the available evidence, finally must be a matter of interpretation, a value judgment based upon their own particular world views. To put the point directly: Economics, as a study of human behavior, cannot avoid value judgments. Struggle as it may, economics as a discipline is never free from ideology.

Although the early economists of the eighteenth and nineteenth centuries—men like Adam Smith, David Ricardo, John Stuart Mill, and especially the heretic Karl Marx—perceived economics as merely part of a broader political economy context, this view had largely been abandoned by practitioners of the "dismal science" by the end of the nineteenth century. In the middle of the twentieth century, the economics profession generally approached "ideology" as if it were a dirty word, unprofessional, or, at the very best, too troublesome to deal with. The emphasis was on theoretical tools, seen as both universal and neutral. All this changed in the 1960s and 1970s when well-known American economists thrust themselves into the powerful debates then sweeping American society. Their views on the war in Vietnam, on poverty, on civil rights, on the extent of government power, on the environmental crisis, on the oil embargo, on the causes of "stagflation," on high technology versus smokestack industries, and much more could be heard regularly on TV talk shows and miniseries or read in the columns of weekly news magazines. Often there was the pretension that this "talking out of church" had little impact on the body of "professional" theory and judgment, but the pretension was unconvincing. For good or ill, the genie was out of the bottle, and the economics profession had again become involved in politics and in recommending political courses of action to pursue economic objectives.

The shrillness of ideological debate has calmed a bit in recent years with the ascendency under the Reagan administration of conservative political and economic doctrines and the general political confusion of American liberalism; however, ideological values continue to shape economic reasoning. Even textbooks that promise to avoid purely political and ethical questions pay at least occasional lip service to the identifiably different policy perspectives of Liberals and Conservatives and usually toss in a separate chapter or two on Radical or Marxist economic thinking.

The significance of all this should not be lost on the beginning student of economics. Such study is not simply an attempt to master a value-free intellectual discipline. The content and application of economic reasoning are determined ultimately by the force of what economists believe, not by an independent and neutral logic. But to say that economics is a matter of opinion is not to say that it is just a study of relatively different ideas: Here's this view and here's that one and each is of equal value. In fact, opinions are not of equal value. There are good opinions and there are bad ones. Different economic ideas have different consequences when adopted as policy. They have different effects, now and in the future. As we confront the various policy solutions proposed to deal with the many crises now gnawing deep into our economy and society, we must make choices. This one seems likely to produce desired outcomes. That one does not. No other situation is consistent with a free and reasoning society. Granted it is a painful situation, since choice always raises doubts and uncertainty and runs the risk of wrong judgment, but it cannot be evaded.

This book is intended to focus on a limited number of the hard choices that we must make. Its basic premise is that economic judgment is fundamentally a matter of learning to choose the best policy solution among all possible solutions. The book further assumes that failure to make this choice is to underestimate the richness and importance of the economic ideas we learn and to be blind to the fact that ideas and analysis do indeed apply to the real world of our own lives.

On Sorting Out Ideologies

Assuming that we have been at least partially convincing in our argument that economic analysis is permeated by ideological judgment, we now turn to examine the varieties of ideology common to American economic thought.

In general, we may characterize the ideological position of contemporary economics and economists as Conservative, Liberal, or Radical. These, the same handy categories that evening newscasters use to describe political positions, presumably have some meaning to people. The trouble with labels, though, is that they can mean a great deal and, at the same time, nothing at all. At a distance the various political colors of Conservative, Liberal, and Radical banners are vividly different. Close up, though, the distinctiveness blurs, and what seemed obvious differences are not so clear. For instance, there is probably *not* a strictly Liberal position on every economic issue, nor are all the economists who might be generally termed "Liberal" in consistent agreement. The same is true in the case of many Radical or Conservative positions as well. Unless we maintain a certain open-endedness in our categorizing of positions, the discussion of ideological differences will be overly simple and much too rigid. Therefore, the following generalizations and applications of ideological typologies will attempt to isolate and identify only "representative" positions. By doing this we can at least focus on the differences at the center rather than on the fuzziness at the fringes of schools of thought.

We are still left with a problem. How do you specify an ideological position? Can you define a Radical or a Liberal or a Conservative position? The answer here is simple enough. As the British economist Joan Robinson once observed, an ideology is like an elephant—you can't define an elephant, but you should know one when you see it. Moreover, you should know the difference between an elephant and a horse or a cow without having to resort to definitions.

There is a general framework of thought within each of the three ideological schools by which we can recognize them. Thus, we will not "define" the schools but merely describe the salient characteristics of each. In all the following, the reader is urged to remember that there are many varieties of elephants. Our specification of a particular ideological view on any issue is a representative model—a kind of average-looking elephant (or horse or cow). Thus the Conservative view offered on the problem of federal deficits, for instance, will probably not encompass all Conservative thought on this question. However, it should be sufficiently representative so that the basic Conservative paradigm, or world view, can be distinguished from the Radical or Liberal argument. Where truly important divisions within an ideological paradigm exist, the divisions will be appropriately noted and discussed.

THE CONSERVATIVE PARADIGM

What is usually labeled the Conservative position in economic thought and policy making was not always "conservative." Conservative ideas may be traced to quite radical origins. The forebears of modern Conservative thought—among them England's Adam Smith (1723–1790)—were not interested in "conserving" the economic order they knew but in destroying it. In 1776, when Smith wrote his classic *Wealth of Nations*, England was organized under a more or less closed economic system of monopoly rights, trade restriction, and constant government interference with the marketplace and with an individual's business and private affairs. This system, known as mercantilism, had been dominant in England and, with slight variations, elsewhere on the Continent for over 250 years.

Adam Smith's Legacy Smith's remedy was simple enough: Remove all restrictions on commercial and industrial activity and allow the market to work freely. The philosophical basis of Smith's argument rested on his beliefs that (1) all men had the natural right to obtain and protect their property, (2) all men were by nature materialistic, and (3) all men were rational and would seek, by their own reason, to maximize their material well-being. These individualistic tendencies in men would be tempered by competition in the marketplace. There men would have to compromise with one another to gain any individual satisfaction whatsoever. The overall effect of these compromises would ultimately lead to national as well as individual satisfaction. Competition and self-interest would keep prices down and production high and rising. They also would stimulate product improvement, invention, and steady economic progress. For this to happen, of course, there would have to be a minimum of interference with the free market—no big government, no powerful unions, and no conspiring in trade. Smith's position and that of his contemporaries and followers was known as ''Classical Liberalism.'' The Conservative label now applied to these views seems to have been affixed much later, when Smith's heirs found themselves acting in the defense of a status quo rather than opposing an older order.

Thus modern capitalist economic thought must trace its origins to Adam Smith. While this body of thought has been built upon and modified over the past 200 years, the hand of Adam Smith is evident in every conventional economics textbook. Common sense tells us, however, that a lot has changed since Smith's day. Today business is big. There are labor unions and big government to interfere with his balanced free market of equals. His optimistic view of a naturally growing and expanding system is now replaced by growth problems and by a steady dose of pessimism in most glances toward the future. Nevertheless, modern Conservatives, among contemporary defenders of capitalism, still stand close to the ideals of Adam Smith.

Modern Conservative thought is anchored to two basic philosophic ideas that distinguish it from Liberal and Radical positions. First, the market system and the spirit of competition are central to proper social organization. Second, individual rights and freedoms must be unlimited and uninfringed.

Conservatives oppose any "unnatural" interference in the marketplace. In particular, the Conservative views the growth of big government in capitalist society as the greatest threat to economic progress. Milton Friedman, Nobel laureate and preeminent figure in the Conservative Chicago school, has argued that government has moved from being merely an instrumentality necessary to sustain the economic and social order and become an instrument of oppression. Friedman's prescription for what "ought to be" on the matter of government is clear:

> A government which maintained law and order, defined property rights, served as a means whereby we could modify property rights and other rules of the economic game, adjudicated disputes about the interpretation of the rules, enforced contracts, promoted competition, provided a monetary framework, engaged in activities to counter technical monopolies and to overcome neighborhood effects widely regarded as sufficiently important to justify government intervention, and which supplemented private charity and the private family in protecting the irresponsible, whether madman or child—such a government would clearly have important functions to perform. The consistent liberal is not an anarchist.*

The antigovernment position of Conservatives in fact goes further than merely pointing out the dangers to individual freedom. To Conservatives, the growth of big government itself causes or worsens economic problems. For instance, the growth of elaborate government policies to improve the conditions of labor, such as minimum-wage laws and social security protection, are seen as actually harming labor in general. A wage higher than that determined by the market will provide greater income for some workers, but, the Conservative argument runs, it will reduce the total demand for labor, and thus dump many workers into unemployment. As this example indicates, the Conservative assault on big government is seen not simply as a moral or ethical question but also in terms of alleged economic effects.

Another unifying feature of the representative Conservative argument is its emphasis on individualism and individual freedom. To be sure, there are those in the Conservative tradition who pay only

---

*Milton Friedman, *Capitalism and Freedom* (Chicago: University of Chicago Press, 1962), p. 34.

lip service to this view, but for true Conservatives it is the centerpiece of their logic. As Friedman has expressed it:

> We take freedom of the individual . . . as the ultimate goal in judging social arguments. . . . In a society freedom has nothing to say about what an individual does with his freedom; it is not an all-embracing ethic. Indeed, the major aim of the liberal [here meaning conservative as we use the term] is to leave the ethical problem for the individual to wrestle with.*

Modern Conservatives as a group exhibit a wide variety of special biases. Not all are as articulate or logically consistent as Friedman's Chicago school. Many are identified more readily by what they oppose than what they seem to be for. While big government, in both its microeconomic interferences and its macroeconomic policy making, is the most obvious common enemy, virtually any institutionalized interference with individual choice is at least ceremonially opposed.

Some critics of the Conservative position are quick to point out that most modern-day Conservatives are not quite consistent on the question of individual freedom when they focus on big business. In fact, until comparatively recently, Conservatives usually did demand the end of business concentration. Like all concentrations of power, it was viewed as an infringement upon individual rights. The Austrian economist Joseph Schumpeter argued that "Big Business is a half-way house on the road to Socialism." The American Conservative Henry C. Simons observed in the depressed 1930s that "the great enemy to democracy is monopoly." Accounting for the change to a more accommodating position on big business is not easy. Conservatives seem to offer two basic reasons. First, big business and the so-called monopoly problem have been watched for a long period of time, and the threat of their power subverting freedom is seen as vastly overstated. Second, by far the larger problem is the rise of big government, which is cited as the greatest cause of business inefficiency and monopoly misuse. Another factor that seems implied in Conservative writing is the fear of communism and socialism, both internal and external. To direct an assault on the American business system, even if existing business concentration were a slight impedi-

*Ibid., p. 12.

ment to freedom, would lay that system open to direct Radical attack. How serious this supposed contradiction in Conservative logic really is remains a matter of debate among its critics.

The Recent Resurgence of Conservative Economic Ideas In the United States, until the drab years of the Great Depression, what we now call "Conservative economics" *was* economics, period. Except for an occasional voice challenging the dominant wisdom, usually to little effect, few economists, political leaders, or members of the public at large disagreed greatly with Adam Smith's emphasis on individual freedom and on a free-market economic condition.

The Depression years, however, brought a strong reaction to this kind of political and economic thinking. Many—perhaps most—of the millions of Americans who were out of work in the 1930s and the millions more who hung on to their jobs by their teeth came to believe that a "free" economy was simply one in "free fall." While most staunch Conservatives complained bitterly about the abandoning of market economics and about the "creeping socialism" of Franklin Roosevelt's New Deal, they had few listeners. For thirty-two of the next forty-eight years after FDR's election in 1932, the White House, and usually the Congress, was in "liberal" Democratic hands. For Conservatives, however, perhaps the greater losses were in the universities, where the old free-market "truths" of Adam Smith and his disciples quickly fell out of style. In their place, a generation of professors espoused the virtues of the "new economics" of John Maynard Keynes and the view that a capitalist economy "requires" government intervention to keep it from destroying itself.

Driven to the margins of academic and political influence by the 1970s, the Conservatives seemed in danger of joining the dinosaur and the dodo bird as an extinct species. But as the old Bob Dylan song goes, "The times, they are a-changing." By the late 1970s, in the aftermath of Vietnam and the Watergate scandal and in a period when nothing government did seemed able to control domestic inflation and unemployment problems, there developed a growing popular reaction against government in general. As more and more Americans came to believe that government economic and social interventions were the cause of the nation's maladies, the Conservative ideology took off again under its own power.

In 1980, the Conservative economic and political paradigm succeeded in recapturing the White House. Ronald Reagan became the first president since Herbert Hoover to come to office after a private-sector career. There was no doubting Reagan's philosophical commitment to the principles of a free-enterprise economy.

As might be expected, Conservatives found themselves facing a difficult situation. Implementing a free-market policy was of course much easier to accomplish in argument than in the real world—especially in a world vastly more complex than that envisioned by Adam Smith. "Reaganomics," the popular catchword for the new brand of Conservative economics, was quickly and sorely tested as the economy slipped into a deep recession in late 1981. To both friendly and hostile critics, Conservatives responded that quick solutions were not possible since the economic debris of a half-century needed to be swept aside before the economy could be reconstructed. Despite the fact that Reaganomics proved to be somewhat less than an unqualified success, Reagan easily defeated Walter Mondale, a liberal Democratic challenger, in 1984. More important from our perspective, a wide range of Conservative economic ideas that had been shunned in serious political and economic debates for over forty years had again made their way back into the economics textbooks.

THE LIBERAL PARADIGM

According to a national opinion poll, Americans tend to associate the term *Liberal* with big government, Franklin Roosevelt, labor unions, and welfare. Time was, not too long ago, when "Liberal" stood not just as a proud appellation but seemed fairly to characterize the natural drift of the whole country. At the height of his popularity and before the Vietnam War toppled his administration, Lyndon Johnson, speaking of the new "Liberal" consensus, observed:

> After years of ideological controversy, we have grown used to the new relationship between government, households, business, labor and agriculture. The tired slogans that made constructive discourse difficult have lost their meaning for most Americans. It has become abundantly clear that our society wants neither to turn backward the clock of his-

tory nor to discuss the present problems in a doctrinaire or partisan spirit.*

Although what we will identify as the "Liberal" position in American economic thought probably still dominates the teaching and practice of economic reasoning (as we shall see, even some Conservatives have adopted elements of the Liberal analysis), the Liberal argument is undergoing considerable changes. The changes, however, are more cosmetic than basic, and the central contours of Liberal belief are still visible.

The "Interventionist" Faith Whereas Conservatives and Radicals are comparatively easily identified by a representative position, Liberals are more difficult. In terms of public policy positions, the Liberal spectrum ranges all the way from those favoring a very moderate level of government intervention to those advocating broad government planning of the economy.

Despite the great distance between the defining poles of Liberal thought, several basic points can be stated as unique to the Liberal paradigm. First, like their Conservative counterparts, Liberals are defenders of the principle of private property and the business system. These, however, are not categorical rights, as we observed in the Conservative case. Individual claims to property or the ability to act freely in the marketplace are subject to the second Liberal principle—that social welfare and the maintenance of the entire economy supersede individual interest. In a vicious condemnation of what we would presently call the Conservative position, John Maynard Keynes directly assaulted the philosophical grounds that set the individual over society. Keynes argued:

> It is not true that individuals possess a prescriptive "natural liberty" in their economic activities. There is no "compact" conferring perpetual rights on those who Have or on those who Acquire. The world is not so governed from above that private and social interest always coincide. It is not a correct deduction from the Principles of Economics that enlightened self-interest always operates in the public interest. Nor is it true that self-interest generally is enlightened; more often individuals acting separately to promote their own ends are too ignorant or too weak to attain even these. Experience does not show that individuals, when

*The Economic Report of the President, 1965 (Washington, D.C.: U.S. Government Printing Office, 1965), p. 39.

they make up a social unit, are always less clear-sighted than when they act separately.*

To the Liberal, then, government intervention in, and occasional direct regulation of, aspects of the national economy is neither a violation of principle nor an abridgment of "natural economic law." The benefits to the whole society from intervention simply outweigh any natural right claims. The forms of intervention may vary, but their pragmatic purpose is obvious—to tinker and manipulate in order to produce greater social benefits.

Government intervention and regulation go back several decades in American history. The Progressives of the early twentieth century were the first to support direct government regulation of the economy. Faced with the individual and collective excesses of the giant enterprises of the era of the Robber Barons, the Progressives followed a number of reformist paths in the period from 1900 to 1920. One was the regulation of monopolistic enterprise, to be accomplished either through direct antitrust regulation or by stimulating competition. Pursuit of these policies was entrusted to a new government regulatory agency, the Federal Trade Commission (created in 1914), an expanded Justice Department and court system, and greater state regulatory powers. Second, indirect business regulation was effected by such Progressive developments as legalization of unions, the passage of social legislation at both the federal and state levels, tax reforms, and controls over production (for example, laws against food adulteration)—all of which tended to circumvent the power of business and subject it to the public interest.

Although the legislation and leadership of the administrations of Theodore Roosevelt, William Howard Taft, and Woodrow Wilson went a long way in moderating the old laissez-faire ideology of the previous era, actual interference in business affairs remained slight until the Great Depression. By 1933 perhaps as many as one out of every three Americans was out of work (the official figures said 25 percent), business failures were common, and the specter of total financial and production collapse hung heavy over the whole country. In the bread lines and shantytowns known as "Hoovervilles" as well as on Main Street, there were serious mutterings that the American

*John M. Keynes, "The End of Laissez Faire," in *Essays in Persuasion* (New York: Norton, 1963), p. 68.

business system had failed. Business leaders, who had always enjoyed hero status in the history books and even among ordinary citizens, had become pariahs. Enter at this point Franklin Roosevelt, the New Deal, and the modern formulation of "Liberal" government-business policies. Despite violent attacks upon him from the Conservative media, FDR pragmatically abandoned his own conservative roots and, in a bewildering series of legislative enactments and presidential decrees, laid the foundation of "public interest" criteria for government regulation of the marketplace. *Whatever might work was tried.* The National Recovery Administration (NRA) encouraged industry cartels and price setting. The Tennessee Valley Authority (TVA) was an attempt at publicly owned enterprise. At the Justice Department, Attorney General Thurman Arnold initiated more antitrust actions than all of his predecessors. And a mass of "alphabet agencies" was created to deal with this or that aspect of the Depression.

Intervention to protect labor and extensions of social welfare provisions were not enough to end the Depression. It was the massive spending for World War II that finally restored prosperity. With this prosperity came the steady influence of Keynes, who had argued in the 1930s that only through government fiscal and monetary efforts to keep up the demand for goods and services could prosperity be reached and maintained. Keynes's arguments for government policies to maintain high levels of investment and hence employment and consumer demand became Liberal dogma. To be a Liberal was to be a Keynesian, and vice versa.

Alvin Hansen, Keynes's first and one of his foremost proponents in the United States, could scarcely hide his glee in 1957 as he described the Liberal wedding of Keynesian policies with the older government interventionist position this way:

> Within the last few decades the role of the economist has profoundly changed. And why? The reason is that economics has become operational. It has become operational because we have at long last developed a mixed public–private economy. This society is committed to the welfare state and full employment. The government is firmly in the driver's seat. In such a world, practical policy problems became grist for the mill of economic analysis. Keynes, more than any other economist of our time, has helped to rescue economics from the negative position

to which it had fallen to become once again a science of the Wealth of Nations and the art of Political Economy.*

Despite the Liberal propensity for tinkering—either through selected market intervention or through macro policy action—most Liberals, like Conservatives, still rely upon supply-and-demand analysis to explain prices and market performance. Their differences with Conservatives on the functioning of markets, determination of output, pricing, and so forth lie not so much in describing what is happening as in evaluating how to respond to what is happening. For instance, there is little theoretical difference between Conservatives and Liberals on how prices are determined under monopolistic conditions. However, to the Conservative, the market itself is the best regulator and preventive of monopoly abuse. To the Liberal, monopoly demands government intervention.

Varieties of Liberal Belief As noted before, the Liberal dogma covers a wide spectrum of opinion. Moreover, the Liberal position has shifted somewhat in response to the past decade's economic disappointments. On the extreme "left wing" of the Liberal spectrum, economists such as Robert Heilbroner and John Kenneth Galbraith have argued that capitalism as a system described and analyzed in conventional economic theory simply does not exist any longer. To this group, it is no longer important even to pretend that capitalism works.

Robert Heilbroner points to the crisis within capitalism as basic to capitalism itself. He argues: "The persistent breakdowns of the capitalist economy, whatever their immediate precipitating factors, can all be traced to a single underlying cause. This is the anarchic or planless character of capitalist production."* This planlessness, according to Heilbroner, sets the stage for government to act as a necessary regulator.

To the left-leaning and always iconoclastic John Kenneth Galbraith, who sees problems of technology rather than profit dominating the giant corporation, a more rational atmosphere for decision

*Alvin H. Hansen, *The American Economy* (New York: McGraw-Hill, 1957), p. 175.

*Robert Heilbroner, *The Limits of American Capitalism* (New York: Harper & Row, 1966), p. 88.

making must be created. In brief, the modern firm demands a high order of internal and external planning of output, prices, and capital. The interests of the firm and state become fused in this planning process, and the expanded role of Liberal government in the whole economy and society becomes obvious. While Galbraith currently maintains that he is a socialist, the Liberal outcome of his program is obvious in that (1) he never explicitly takes up the expropriation of private property, and (2) he still accepts a precarious social balance between public and private interest.

While Galbraith's Liberalism leads to the planned economy, most Liberals stop well before this point. Having rejected the logic of self-regulating markets and accepted the realities of giant business enterprise, Liberals unashamedly admit to being pragmatic tinkerers—ever adjusting and interfering with business decision making in an effort to assert the changing "public interest." Yet all this must be done while still respecting basic property rights and due process. Under these arrangements, business regulation amounts to a protection of business itself as well as the equal protection of other interest groups in pluralist American society.

In the not-too-distant past, business itself adapted to and embraced this position. While certain government actions might be opposed, the philosophy of government intervention in the economy was not necessarily seen as antibusiness. The frequent Conservative depiction of most Liberals as being opposed to the business system does not withstand the empirical test. For instance, in 1964 Henry Ford II organized a highly successful businessmen's committee for Liberal Lyndon Johnson while Conservative Barry Goldwater, with Friedman as his advisor, gained little or no big-business support. However, the extent of government regulation soon reached a level that was wholly unacceptable to the private sector. In the late 1960s and early 1970s, a blizzard of environmental, job-safety, consumer-protection, and energy regulations blew out of Washington. Added to what was already on the ground, the new legislative snowfall seemed to many businessmen at the end of the 1970s about to bring American business to a standstill. Many who a decade before frankly feared the economic "freedom" of the Conservative vision now embraced that position.

After nearly a decade of economic distress and in the wake of a growing popular sentiment against government authority as expressed through the Reagan victory, most Liberal "interventionists" are frankly confused. Many can be counted upon to hold on to their old commitment to pragmatic tinkering, especially those whose interests are closely and narrowly tied to special-interest groups—environmentalists, consumer advocates, the poor, minorities, labor unions, and so forth. Even a few business persons, worried about growing foreign competition and concerned about the decline of many of the nation's basic industries, have called for expanded government intervention. Others are beginning to rethink their position on intervention. To this group, it is not a question of abandoning the basic concept of government intervention in the economy—that would be an admission that the Conservatives' view of a self-balancing economy was essentially correct. Rather, the problem is to redefine what kind of intervention is desirable.

More and more, Liberals admit the failure of past interventionist programs: social assistance, the use of regulatory agencies, corporate and personal income tax policies, and many more of the centerpieces of Liberal economic legislation. Many have backed off from their earlier tendency to slap a government bandaid onto any and every economic problem. Others argue simply that the problem is only to find better solutions, not to stop undertaking the problems.

The present-day ambivalence of Liberals on the degree and type of intervention will be evident in our survey of economic issues in this book; nevertheless, this tendency should not be misunderstood. Specific Liberal approaches to problem solving may be debatable, but the essence of Liberal economics remains unchanged: The capitalist economy simply requires pragmatic adjustment from time to time to maintain overall balance and to protect particular elements in the society.

THE RADICAL PARADIGM

Specifying a Radical position would have been no problem a few decades ago. Outside of a handful of Marxist scholars, some socialists left over from the 1920s and 1930s, and a few unconventional muckrakers, there was no functioning Radical tradition in American economic thought. However, the two-sided struggles of the 1960s over racism and poverty at home and the war in Vietnam produced a resurgence of Radical critiques. By the mid 1970s, the Radical caucus within the American Economic Association had forced on that body topics for discussion at annual meetings that directly challenged conventional economic thought. The Union of Radical Political Economics (URPE) could boast over 2,000 members and its own journal. Meanwhile, basic textbooks in economics began to add chapters on "Radical economics."

The Marxist Heritage Radical economics had arrived—but what, precisely, was it? To many non-Radicals, it was simply Marxist economics warmed over, but this explanation, though basically true, is too simple. To be sure, the influence of Marx, the leading critic of capitalism, is pervasive in most Radical critiques. But Radical economics is more than Marx. His analysis of capitalism is over one hundred years old and deals with a very different set of capitalist problems. (In Marx's time, capitalism was only in the beginning stages of industrial development and was still characterized by small entrepreneurs carrying on essentially merchant capitalist undertakings.) With this qualification in mind, we will argue, however, that no study of current Radical thought is possible unless one starts with, or at least touches upon, the ideas of Karl Marx. Although a few iconoclastic Radicals will reject a close association with Marxism, the evidence is overwhelming that Marxist analysis is central to understanding the representative Radical position in America today.

Since the Marxist critique is likely to be less familiar to many readers than the basic arguments of Conservatives or Liberals, it is necessary to be somewhat more detailed in specifying the Radical position. As will be quickly apparent, the Radical world view rests on greatly different assumptions about the economic and social order than those of the Conservatives and the Liberals.

According to Marx's view, the value of a commodity reflects the real labor time necessary to produce it. However, under capitalism, workers lack control of their labor, selling it as they must to capitalists. The workers receive only a fraction of the value they create— according to Marx, only an amount sufficient in the long run to permit subsistence. The rest of the value—what Marx calls "surplus value"—is retained by capitalists as the source of their profits and for the accumulation of capital that will increase both future production and future profit. As the appropriation of surplus value proceeds, with the steady transference of living labor into capital (what Marx called "dead labor"), capitalists face an emerging crisis. With more and more of their production costs reflecting their growing dependence upon capital (machines) and with surplus labor value their only source of profit, capitalists are confronted with the reality of not being able to expand surplus appropriation. Unless they are able to increase their exploitation of labor—getting more output for the same, or less, wages paid—they face a falling rate of profit on their growing capital investment. Worse still, with workers' relatively falling wages and capitalists' relatively increasing capacity to produce, there is a growing tendency for the entire capitalist system to produce more goods than it can in fact sell.

These trends set certain systemic tendencies in motion. Out of the chaos of capitalist competitive struggles for profits in a limited market there develops a drive toward "concentration and centralization." In other words, the size of businesses grows and the number of enterprises shrinks. However, the problems of the falling rate of profit and chronic overproduction create violent fluctuations in the business cycle. Each depression points ever more clearly toward capitalist economic collapse. Meanwhile, among the increasingly impoverished workers, there is a steady growth of a "reserve army of unemployed"—workers who are now unemployable as production decreases. Simultaneously, increasing misery generates class consciousness and revolutionary activity among the working class. As the economic disintegration of capitalist institutions worsens, the subjective consciousness of workers grows to the point where they successfully overthrow the capitalist system. In the new society, the workers themselves take control of the production process, and accumulation for the interest of a narrow capitalist class ceases.

The Modern Restatement of Marx   Of necessity, the modern Radical's view of the world must lack the finality of Marx's predictions. Quite simply, the capitalist system has not self-destructed and, in fact, in a good many respects is stronger and more aggressive than it was in Marx's day. Although the modern-day Radical may still agree with Marx's long-run predictions about the ultimate self-destructiveness of the capitalist order, the fact is that *relevant* Radicals must deal with the world as it is. While the broad categories of Marx's analysis are retained in a general way, Radical thought must focus on real-world, present-day conditions of capitalist society and present an analysis that gets beyond merely asserting the Marxist scenario for capitalist collapse. Indeed, useful economic analysis must be offered in examining contemporary problems.

The beginning point for modern Radical critiques, as it was also for Marx over a hundred years ago, is the unquenchable capitalist thirst for profits. This central organizing objective of all capitalist systems determines everything else within those systems. The Radical analysis begins with a simple proposition about how capitalists understand market activity:

Total sales = total cost of materials and machinery used up in production + total wages and salaries paid + (− in the case of losses) total profits

Such a general view of sales, costs, and profits is, thus far, perfectly consistent with traditional accounting concepts acceptable to any Conservative or Liberal. However, the Radical's analytic mission becomes clearer when the proposition is reformulated:

Total profits = total sales − total cost of materials and machinery used up in production − total wages and salaries paid

It now becomes evident that increasing profits depends on three general conditions: (1) that sales rise, *ceteris paribus* (all things being equal); (2) that production costs (composed of wage costs and material and machinery costs) decline, *ceteris paribus*; or (3) that sales increases at least exceed production cost increases. The capitalist, according to the Radical argument, is not simply interested in total profits but also in the "rate of profit," or the ratio of profits to the amount of capital the capitalist has invested.

With capitalist eyes focused on raising profits or raising profit rates, it becomes clear to Radicals what individual economic policies and strategies will be advanced by capitalists: *Every effort will be made to keep costs low,* such as reducing wage rates, speeding up the production line, introducing so-called labor-saving machines, seeking cheaper (often foreign) sources of labor and materials, and minimizing outlays for waste treatment and environmental maintenance. At the same time, *efforts will be made to keep prices high,* in particular through the development of monopolistic price-making power on both a national and an international scale. In all these activities, capitalists will make every effort to use government economic intervention to their own advantage—both in domestic markets and in expanding capitalist hegemony into the world.

However, the efforts of individual capitalists—either on their own or aided by government—to expand profit produces, taking the system as a whole, a crisis in obtaining profits. For instance, the capitalist goals of keeping wages low and prices high must lead to situations where workers as consumers simply cannot clear the market of available goods. Accordingly, the aggregate economy deteriorates into periodic recession or depression, with rising unemployment among workers and falling profits for capitalists. With capitalist support, a variety of government monetary and fiscal efforts may be employed to offset these ups and downs in the capitalist business cycle—in particular to improve the profit and profit-rate situations of capitalist enterprises. However, so-called mixed capitalism (a mixture of private-sector and government planning of the economy) cannot overcome the fundamental contradictions of a dominantly private, production-for-profit economy. And, of course, with the expansion of capitalism throughout most of the world, the capitalist crisis takes on international proportions. Quite as Marx predicted, the general economic crises deepen and occur more frequently. The search for profit becomes more frantic and more destructive to the lives of ever greater numbers of people living under capitalist hegemony throughout the world.

From the Radical point of view, periodic crisis in capitalism is not the result of excessive tinkering with the market system, as Conservatives claim; nor will the tendency toward crisis be contained by Liberal interventionism. Periodic and deepening crisis *is* capitalism.

Radical analysis is, of course, more penetrating than this short résumé can indicate. One further point that should be examined briefly is Marx's view of the relationship between a society's organization for production and its social relations. To Marx, capitalism was more than an economic system. Private values, religion, the family, the educational system, and political structures were all shaped by capitalist class domination and by the goal of production for private profit. It is important to recognize this tenet in any discussion of how Marxists—or Radicals with a Marxist orientation—approach contemporary social and economic problems. Marxists do not separate economics from politics or private belief. For instance, racism cannot be abstracted to the level of an ethical question. Its roots are seen in the capitalist production process. Nor is the state ever viewed as a neutrality able to act without class bias. Bourgeois democracy as we know it is seen simply as a mask for class domination.

Marx, in his early writings before his great work, *Capital*, had emphasized the "qualitative" exploitation of capitalism. Modern Radicals have revitalized this early Marx in their "quality of life" assaults on the present order. In these they emphasize the problems of worker alienation, commodity fetishism, and the wasteful and useless production of modern capitalism. The human or social problems of modern life are seen as rooted in the way the whole society is geared to produce more and more profits.

In addition to their Marxist heritage, modern Radicals derive much of their impulse from what they see as the apparent failure of Liberalism. Liberal promises to pursue policies of general social improvement are perceived as actions to protect only *some* interest groups. In general, those benefiting under Liberal arrangements are seen as those who have always gained. The corporation is not controlled. It is more powerful than ever. Rule by elites has not ended, nor have the elites changed. Moreover, the national goals of the Liberal ethic—to improve our overall national well-being—have stimulated the exploitation of poor nations, continued the cold war, and increased the militarization of the economy.

The Question of Relevance Quite obviously, the Marxist prediction of capitalism's final collapse has not yet come to pass. For critics of the Radical position, this fact, along with certain internal analytic problems, is quite sufficient to consign their critique to the garbage heap. Such a view is somewhat unenlightened. First of all, Marx's ideas in one form or another are more prominent in the world today than the other two ideologies discussed here. Second, Marxism—at least as American Radical scholars have developed and used it—is more a way of looking at how our economy works than a prophecy of things to come. It is the technique of analysis rather than the century-old "truth" of Marx's specific analysis that counts.

As noted before, not all Radicals subscribe to all Marxist doctrine, but Marxism in one form or another remains the central element of the Radical challenge. Marx's fundamental contention that the system of private production must be changed remains the badge of membership in the Radical ranks. This sets Radicals apart from mainstream Conservative and Liberal economists.

Critics of Radicalism usually point out that Radical analyses are hopelessly negativistic. Radicals, they say, describe the problems of capitalism without offering a solution other than the end of the whole system. While there is much truth to this charge, we shall see in the following sections that indeed some solutions are offered. But even if their program were vague, Radicals would argue that their greatest contribution is in revealing the truth of the capitalist system.

Somewhat like the Liberals, Radical theorists have been victimized lately by real-world events. The economic crunch of the 1970s and the recent heating up of the cold war between the USSR and the USA propelled Americans toward Conservative economic values rather than toward the left. Moreover, the old Radical constituencies either disappeared, as in the case of the antiwar youth of the 1960s and 1970s, or have been eroded, as in the case of environmental and consumer advocacy. Nevertheless, the force of an idea is not dependent upon the number of true believers. Were that the case, Conservative economic doctrine would have disappeared twenty years ago. Despite lessened political influence, modern Radical economic thought still looms as a logically important alternative to the more broadly supported Conservative and Liberal paradigms.

Applying the Analysis to the Issues

We have identified representative paradigms; now we will put them to use. The following selected issues by no means exhaust the economic and political crises troubling the nation; nevertheless, this book still should provide a good-sized sampling of the social agenda confronting us. The issues presented here were selected because of their immediacy and representativeness in illustrating the diverse ideological approaches of Conservative, Liberal, and Radical economic analyses.

In each of the following issues, the representative paradigms are presented in a *first-person advocacy approach*. The reader might do well to regard the arguments like those in a debate. As in a debate, one should be careful to distinguish between substantive differences and mere logical or debating strategies. Thus some points may be quite convincing while others seem shallow. However, the reader should remember that, shallow or profound, these are representative political economic arguments advanced by various economic schools.

The sequence in presenting the paradigms is consistent throughout the text: first Conservative, then Liberal, then Radical. In terms of the logical and historical development of contemporary economic ideologies, this sequence is most sensible; however, it is certainly not necessary to read the arguments in this order. Each one stands by itself. Nor is any ideological position intentionally set out as a straw man in any debate.

Readers should look at each position critically. They should test their own familiarity with economic concepts and their common sense against what they read in any representative case. Finally, of course, as students of economics and as citizens, they must make their own decisions. They determine who, if anyone, is the winner of the debate.

Because of space limitations, the representative arguments are brief, and some important ideas have been boiled down to a very few sentences. Also, within each of the three major positions there is a wide variety of arguments, which may sometimes be at variance with one another. Conservatives, Liberals, and Radicals disagree among themselves on specific analyses and programs. For the sake of simplicity, we have chosen not to emphasize these differences but arbitrarily (although after much thought) have tried to select the most representative arguments. Each paradigm's discussion of an issue presents a critique of present public policy and, usually, a specific program proposal.

In all of the arguments, the factual and empirical evidence offered has been checked for accuracy. It is instructive in itself that, given the nature of economic "facts," they can be marshaled to "prove" a great variety of different ideological positions. Different or even similar evidence supports different truths, depending on the truth we wish to prove.

PART 2

PROBLEMS OF AGGREGATE ECONOMIC POLICY

Part 2 focuses on issues that are primarily *macroeconomic* in origin. In other words, our attention will be directed to issues affecting the economy as a whole and to variables affecting its aggregate economic performance. Specifically, we shall examine such problem areas as business cycle behavior, stabilization policy, the federal deficit, unemployment, the military and social budgets, international trade and money policy, and centralized economic planning.

ISSUE 1

Business Fluctuations
Are We Depression-proof?

We have nothing to fear but fear itself.

Franklin Roosevelt, 1933

My position is essentially unchanged since 1979. I don't see three or four years of grass growing on Main Street, of debt deflation, of cascading dominoes of bankruptcies. I don't see the dice loaded in that direction.

Paul A. Samuelson,
Nobel laureate, MIT, 1982

The predictors of doom were dead wrong. This administration has replaced the gloomy talk of recession with an economy that is strong and getting stronger every day.

Donald Regan, presidential advisor, 1985

Reagan is putting up a notable effort to have another Great Depression. But the important structural and psychological safeguards built up since 1929 are still in place.

John Kenneth Galbraith,
Harvard University, 1982

In world market crisis, the contradictions and antagonisms of bourgeois production break through to the surface. But instead of investigating the nature of the . . . catastrophe, the apologists content themselves with denying the catastrophe itself.

Karl Marx, 1867

THE PROBLEM

Although the Great Depression is no longer part of "recent American history" and is remembered only dimly by a comparative handful of Americans, its impact remains very great among economic thinkers. The years from the stock market crash of 1929 to the beginning of World War II were a crucial watershed for modern economic policy. Depression, the specter of depression, and, most important, the ability to avoid any future depressions have since held the attention of macroeconomic policy makers.

The domination of modern economic thought by events and developments now nearly half a century old is understandable when the severity of this "Great Rupture" in American history is examined. Between 1929 and 1933, the gross national product (the nation's annual output of goods and services) was sliced almost in half. Unemployment, which had averaged about 13 percent in 1929, soared to 24.9 percent by 1933. Unemployment for 1933 totaled 13 million men and women, but this figure was deceiving since several times that amount, perhaps 65 percent of the labor force, suffered some unemployment or could obtain only part-time work. On the business side, before-tax corporate profits fell from a record $11 billion in 1929 to an operating loss of $1.2 billion four years later, and industrial production declined by more than 45 percent.

Historians have documented the wrenching effect of the Depression on institutions and values. However great the changes in modes of American thought and behavior, none were more profound than those in economic thinking and practice. Before Black Tuesday's stock market collapse (October 29, 1929) and the crisis that followed, conventional economic wisdom unashamedly espoused the virtues of laissez-faire. The economy was to operate freely. Although this meant the periodic toleration of bad times as business activity occasionally slowed, these downturns were offset by succeeding periods of expansion and prosperity. Left alone, economic analysis held, the economy would right itself and, over time, move upward to new, higher levels of output, employment, and real income.

But recovery was not spontaneous in the Great Depression, and for good or ill, the orthodox belief in the self-regulating business cycle fell from favor. Ruminating on the worldwide depression in England, John Maynard Keynes concluded it was time to clear the intellectual stage of all the old furniture of economic orthodoxy. In 1936, his *General Theory of Employment, Interest, and Money* proclaimed that capitalist economic institutions were not self-balancing mechanisms but instead tended toward chronic stagnation. This situation required action by governments through fiscal and monetary policy to forestall collapse. The solution: Raise aggregate demand for goods, thereby putting to work unemployed people and closed plants. Not given to modesty, Keynes correctly warned his readers that his ideas would change the way people thought about modern capitalist economies. And they did, as Keynes' New Economics became the new dominant wisdom in economic matters.

For most of the first three decades after World War II, Keynesian orthodoxy reigned. The Keynesian view that periodic slumps in the economy could and should be offset by government efforts to stimulate the demand for goods went virtually unquestioned, and many economists began to think and act like fluctuations in business activity were only a feature of the past, pre-Keynesian era. However, events in the mid-1970s began to prompt a reexamination of the New Economics. Although no "Great Depression" developed, the economy did stagger through a "Great Stagflation" as economic growth slowed, unemployment rates rose, and price inflation gnawed deep into the economy's innards. For the generations that had not experienced the crisis after 1929, the stagflationary years of the 1970s became the great shaping economic event of their time. The depression years of the 1930s were far distant; the "Great Rupture" was really the middle and late 1970s.

To many, Liberal Keynesian orthodoxy seemed unable to deal with the new crisis. Armed with a revitalized analysis of the macroeconomy, Conservatives convincingly argued that current economic problems were the actual result of Keynesians' myopic focus on only the demand-management activities of government and their failure to understand the central importance of the productive activities of the private sector, what quickly became known as the "supply side."

On platforms firmly based on a new "supply side" analysis, Conservative Ronald Reagan was swept into the White House in 1980 and returned again in 1984. Reagan victories, however, did not produce a complete repudiation of Lord Keynes. Although inflation slowed after 1981 and the economy revived a bit by the mid-1980s, few objective thinkers could state with much certainty that this had been the direct result of a Conservative "revolution" in economic thinking. To be sure, the Conservatives had introduced a supply-side focus not present in the Keynesian critique, and the earlier simplistic Keynesian solutions to many economic problems had shown themselves to be much less adequate than their defenders understood. However, it was by no means universally agreed that the new supply-side approaches had once and for all shelved the old economic worry of whether or not another Great Depression was possible.

SYNOPSIS. The Conservative position maintains that depression and protracted economic stagnation are not central to capitalist economic systems and that the business cycle downturn after 1929 was worsened, not moderated, by government intervention in the economy. Liberals argue that only through vigorous and active countercyclical policies by government can the economy's natural propensity toward recession and depression be controlled. To Radicals, crisis and depression are quite natural to production-for-profit systems, and although crises may be delayed by governmental actions, they cannot be eliminated in the long run.

Anticipating the Arguments

- On what grounds do Conservatives argue that Liberals and Radicals have failed to prove their case that capitalism "naturally" tends toward protracted periods of economic stagnation? How do they account for economic downturns?

- In what ways did the Keynesian critique depart from the "conventional wisdom" of the 1930s?

- In what ways does the Radical scenario of capitalism's "chronic tendency toward crisis" differ from the Liberal Keynesian view?

The Conservative Argument

For most of the past half century, the great majority of American and other Western economists have labored under a grand delusion about the means by which the national economy may be insulated from recurring economic collapse. The deep fracture of the 1930s caused the virtual abandonment of time-proven economic wisdom. The fear of a return to general depression conditions has simply continued to dominate the popular imagination and the thinking of many economists.

Such worries, however, rather than reflecting the real significance of events, attest to the persuasiveness of myth over reality. To put matters directly, most of what is believed about the causes of the Depression is wrong. More important, the body of economic policy developed to make us depression-proof is dangerously irrelevant, constructed to deal with a problem that never existed. Alas, the cumbersome structure of government intervention in the economy through countercyclical fiscal and monetary policy and the consequent chilling economic effect of bloated government budgets and deficits have been unnecessary. Indeed, government intervention is more of a threat to stability than a bulwark.

ON MISREADING THE SIGNIFICANCE AND CAUSES OF THE GREAT DEPRESSION

Contrary to popular economic beliefs, the initial business downturn between 1929 and 1930 was not in itself a unique event. As most economists know but sometimes overlook, the general economic performance of the United States, both before the Great Depression and after (even with the tools of the new economists), has followed a cyclical course. Indeed, the expansion–contraction rhythm of economic affairs had fascinated many students of business cycles long before the Depression of the 1930s. Business contractions had appeared at intervals of about eight to twelve years, each eventually succeeded by a counteracting stage of growth and prosperity. Economists offered a variety of explanations for such cyclical behavior, including new inventions, changes in investment or consumer behavior, and even sunspot activity. But before the 1930s, few, except perhaps the Marxists committed to the destruction of the system, held that business contraction could become a permanent state of affairs. Just as surely as the business cycle turned downward, it would sooner or later turn upward.

This, however, did not happen in 1929–1930, and to obtain a clearer understanding of modern-day economic tendencies, we must ask why.

According to the zealots who quickly snatched up John Maynard Keynes' ideas and perverted them to their own uses, the depression of the 1930s was not merely a periodic movement within the business cycle. Instead, it was a problem of chronic "stagnation," a situation in which the economy could no longer maintain high levels of employment and output because of the inadequacy of business investment. In short, depression had become a permanent state of affairs.

Such a situation, according to Keynes' followers, demanded firm action. First, the economy would have to be managed by government since Treasury and monetary authorities could no longer count on the natural bottoming out of a depression. Second, government would have to act to "stimulate demand"—to increase consumer spending and business investment. Third, this demand stimulation would probably have to come from enlarged state expenditures, purposely unbalanced budgets and deficit spending for public goods, and transfer payments to businesses and individuals.

Thus began the "modern" period of economic thought. The epoch of laissez-faire was to be closed, with government replacing private accumulation and private instincts as the driving force of the economic system. Never mind the past spectacular performance of the private and open economy in building the nation. Never mind the implied assaults upon individual economic freedom and choice that were the underpinnings of political freedom in the United States. Lord Keynes and his followers had determined that these now were outmoded beliefs and that only through massive government intervention in the economy could survival be assured.

A BETTER INTERPRETATION

Ordinarily, the best test for a hypothesis that interprets a set of events is to ask whether the hypothesis adequately explains the situation and is the best explanation possible. Applying this rule to the Keynesian critique, we find it wanting.

First, there is no evidence to support the idea that the Great Depression was, at its beginning in 1929, exceptional or that it differed markedly from past business downturns. Therefore, there is nothing to support the Keynesian belief that depression had become a permanent and congenital economic condition by the 1930s. What we do know, however, is that the depressed business conditions were worsened by the money policy actions of the Federal Reserve Board, the government authority charged with maintenance of the nation's money and banking system. The Fed succeeded in transforming the difficulties of an excessively careless epoch of stock market speculation, coupled with an ordinary downturn in the business cycle, into an economic catastrophe of the first magnitude.

Lowering interest rates had always served to bring forth new investment and stimulate recovery in past downturns. However, reacting to the speculative bull market, the Fed had pursued a tight money policy even when it was apparent in early 1929 that a business downturn was forming. With high interest rates discouraging new business borrowing and reducing the stock of money (the money supply), business investment and consumer buying sagged even before the stock market collapsed. This was the Fed's first mistake. Its second came in December 1930 when the Bank of the United States in New York City closed its doors. Although it was an ordinary commercial bank, many people believed it to be an official government bank, and panic set in. Depositors in New York City and elsewhere rushed to withdraw their savings. Bank after bank faced liquidity crises. Unable to meet depositors' demands, banks began to fall like a line of dominoes. Meanwhile, the Fed, created in 1914 for just such an emergency, failed to take any action to improve bank liquidity. In fact, its next action was simply disastrous. In September 1931, as economic and financial problems spread worldwide and more and more gold was drained from the United States, the Fed raised interest rates in an attempt to stop the overseas flow of gold. Banks, now unable to borrow from the Fed to meet their customers' demands for cash (because of the high interest rates), had no recourse but to fold. Fourteen hundred closed their doors in three months, and the nation's money supply (consisting largely of demand deposits) fell by 12 percent. Meanwhile, on the business side, high interest rates discouraged new investment, and consumer spending fell as the money supply contracted. An ordinary depression had been transformed into an unprecedented financial crisis and, in turn, a near-complete prostration of business.

One other misguided economic action deserves special note: passage in 1930 of the protectionist Smoot-Hawley Tariff. Under pressure from businesses seeking to protect domestic markets from foreign competition, the Hoover administration, caught up in the anxiety following the market crash, encouraged Congress to pass a tariff that established the highest duties on imported goods in American history. Predictably, our protectionism was quickly matched by similar actions by our trading partners, and, while we were protected from imports, we soon found it impossible to sell our products overseas.

The foregoing analysis differs sharply from the Keynesian stagnationist approach. While the Keynesians are partially correct that the Depression did finally become a matter of insufficient aggregate demand, that happened only after and as a result of the failure of the Federal Reserve System and the passage of Smoot-Hawley. Rather than the economy manifesting some sinister and fatal stagnationist flaw, the evidence suggests that the Great Depression was largely accidental. That being the case, there is no proven analytical foundation for the Keynesian prescription that only through massive government intervention can a free-enterprise economy be kept afloat. Ironically, when we focus on the critical failures of monetary policy and tariff policy between 1929 and 1933, we find the reverse of the Keynesian analysis to be true: that government actions (through the Fed and Smoot-Hawley) in fact caused the Great Depression.

The worsening and deepening of the Depression after 1933 was also the result of government activity. Liberal defenders of Franklin Roosevelt like to depict the New Deal as an experimental and pragmatic program to "prime" the economy. Not yet convinced by the Keynesian arguments, FDR is usually presented as doing too little with countercyclical policy to get things going (until the government spending boom of World War II). This interpretation of the New Deal period of the Great Depression is guilty of a serious error of omission.

FDR's antidepression strategy, Keynesian or not, was antibusiness and antibanker. The president's public addresses identified these groups as both the cause of the Depression and the reason why his own policies had not turned the economic tide. His attempts to increase regulatory agency power, to insert government in the pricing mechanism, to reform the banking community, and especially to reform the Supreme Court when it threw out key pieces of his interventionist legislation created considerable business uncertainty. Within such a charged political atmosphere, business expectations, key to the undertaking of new investment and critical to recovery, remained essentially negative. Thus the interventionist policies of the New Deal tended to deepen and broaden the already critical business depression.

THE PAINFUL LEGACY OF THE DEPRESSION

The passing of the Depression did not signal the passing of Keynesian ideas; indeed, it only marked the beginning of a long era of wrongheaded economic thought and policy. The victory of the Keynesian analysis led to the building of ever more elaborate theories to justify the enlargement of the government sector. The size of federal spending grew, and the extent of fiscal and monetary manipulation of business activity was enlarged. For decades, beginning students of economics were taught, as if it were received religious truth, that deficits do not matter, that the growth of the public sector is healthy, and that the macro performance of the economy can be insulated from depression and "fine-tuned" to produce desired levels of output, employment, and price stability both instantaneously and in the long run.

By the 1970s, however, the basic flaws of such an analysis were becoming uncomfortably evident as the nation slipped into a decade of inflation, unemployment, and disappointing growth. The Keynesian emphasis on "maintaining demand" meant neglecting and even restricting the production or supply side of the economy. As we shall see in subsequent issues, it led by the 1970s to an explosion of the federal debt, which in turn triggered an inflationary spiral that discouraged savings and slowed business investment. Incorrectly deciding that business had caused the depression led naturally enough to forgetting that business was in fact the very foundation of the economy. The situation was a bit like concluding that the health of the goose that laid the golden eggs would be improved by increasing the demand for eggs.

Looking back over the years of Keynesian dominance, with its patchwork of countercyclical and income-redistribution programs, George Gilder has observed:

> When government gives welfare, unemployment payments, and public service jobs in quantities that deter productive work, and when it raises

taxes on profitable enterprises to pay for them, demand declines. In fact, nearly all programs that are advocated [by Keynesian economists] . . . in actuality reduce demand by undermining the production from which all real demand derives. . . . This is the essential insight of supply side economics. Government cannot significantly affect real aggregate demand through policies of taxing and spending.*

At best, the demand-side management efforts of the Keynesians amount to a "zero-sum" game, merely shifting the earnings of some to others. At worst, as we shall see in the next issue, Keynesian fiscal and monetary policy ideas drive the economy downward. The growing political, professional, and even popular reaction against "depression economics" in the 1980s is a heartening development.

ARE WE REALLY DEPRESSION-PROOF?

Turning to the original question of whether or not another Great Depression is possible, the Conservative position, although similar to the Liberal Keynesian position in giving a negative response, should be seen in light of its own assumptions. First, a massive depression is not the natural outcome of a free enterprise economy. Second, the elaborate policy tools developed to "insulate" the economy from depression are both unjustified and inherently dangerous. Third, the fact that we have not experienced a serious depression since the 1930s should not be accepted as proof that Keynesian macro policy has worked. Rather, it might just as easily prove that the private economy is basically durable and adaptable—even with Keynesian roadblocks thrown in its way.

Thus we can conclude that another Great Depression is not inevitable unless, of course, we continue to rely on mistaken interpretations and cures in the formation of public policy. The "cures" we learned from the last depression are a far greater menace to future stability than anything else on the horizon.

The Liberal Argument

Naturally, it must be conceded that the "stagflationary" events of the 1970s demonstrated that a too narrow Keynesianism has limitations in dealing with *all* of the problems of the modern economy;

*George Gilder, *Wealth and Poverty* (New York: Bantam Books, 1981), pp. 62–63.

however, such events should not be misread. The recent economic difficulties of unemployment *plus* inflation do not prove the essential Keynesian critique to be in error. The absence of self-adjusting and self-regulating mechanisms in a laissez-faire capitalist economy is just as true today as in the 1930s. Similarly, the tendency of mature capitalist systems to tend toward stagnation remains as much a characteristic as ever. Whatever the benefits of emphasizing the production side of the economy, and most Liberals would admit that some benefits have been obtained from the recent supply-side debate, this does not amount to a proof that Keynes' basic analysis should be abandoned in favor of a return to the laissez-faire assumptions of a bygone and discredited era.

THE COLLAPSE OF ORTHODOX IDEAS IN THE 1930s

The prevailing economic view in 1929 was that the economy was a "natural," self-adjusting mechanism. Wages, interest, and rents were paid to individuals according to the value of their contributions to national output. Such payments were, over time, equitable and just rewards for work and risk. The general mode of economic activity was pure competition. Interferences in the economy, whether by government, labor unions, or collusive business practice, were condemned. The "economy" was thus described and analyzed theoretically in terms of an open laissez-faire system. To be sure, periodic downturns in the national economy were possible, just as periodic stickiness in wages, savings, and business investment were possible. However, the focus was on the long haul, and, over time, such deviations were thought to be self-correcting.

Within this general economic structure, economists of the traditional order based their analysis of the national economy on a four-cornered foundation. First, there would be no long-run overproduction of goods (or, to look at it from the other side, no long-run underconsumption). This was true because payments to the producers, labor, business, and so forth, were always equal to the value of the goods produced. As the nineteenth-century French economist Jean Baptiste Say had put it in what has since come to be known as Say's law, "Supply creates its own demand."

Second, and following from the first point, there could be, again in the long run, no such thing as involuntary unemployment. With flexible wages and prices, there would always be sufficient work at any given wage level to employ all those willing to work at that wage. Individuals who chose not to work at a particular wage (supposedly because they valued leisure more) were not "unemployed" at all.

Third, through free and flexible interest rates, private savings would be just enough to meet the investment (or borrowing) needs of businesses. If business sought greater investment, interest rates would rise, people would choose to save more, and funds would become available for business expansion. This, in turn, would create jobs, raise wages, and stimulate balanced economic growth.

Fourth, the level of prices in the society were determined by the rate of growth of the money supply. An increase in money would stimulate spending and demand for goods, which would raise market prices. A decrease in money would lower prices.

To the orthodox, these theories offered policy solutions to the periodic downturns in the economy. If business output exceeded consumer demand, wait! Prices would fall to clear the market of goods. Wages would fall, and the number of workers seeking employment would be reduced until an equilibrium wage was reached. Interest rates would fall, and individuals would shift savings to consumption. With lower interest rates and increasing consumption, business would again invest. Public policy within such a self-balancing economic order could be described quite easily: Do nothing!

As the international economy continued to inch downward after 1929, John Maynard Keynes began to rethink the orthodox analysis and reach his own conclusion on the evidence at hand. First of all, he observed that the automaticity of Say's law was unfounded. Indeed, it was possible for overproduction or underconsumption to develop if individuals hold money rather than save it (lend it to borrowers). Second, wages were not, in the real world, freely flexible. Business could and did keep prices up and laid off workers while awaiting the sale of inventories. The alternatives available to workers were not lower wages or leisure but simply increased unemployment. Third, lowered interest rates did not induce business investment at a time of overproduction. Business, with goods on hand, would be unlikely to produce more goods even if the cost of borrowing were near zero.

Thus in the Keynesian analysis, the "short-run" business fluctuations of the economy could become very long indeed. The self-correcting nature of the economy was an incorrect premise. And squaring with the real evidence that continued to build after the early 1930s, it was possible to have a continuing low level of output that left large numbers of workers and factories idle. Indeed, it was not only possible, it was quite natural in an unregulated economic system.

THE KEYNESIAN SOLUTION

Keynes' objective in his *General Theory* was to lay out the path to a high-employment economy. His approach emphasized aggregate rather than microeconomic aspects, as orthodox analysts did. First, aggregate levels of employment depended upon the total demand for goods, including consumer purchase of goods and business investment as well as government spending. Second, the primary culprit in the cyclical downturn of an economy was the activity of investors, since it is through changes in investment outlays that changes in total demand for goods and services are affected most directly. Consumer spending was a fairly constant function of total income, with consumer outlays rising and falling directly as national income fluctuated. Government spending was small, and, in depression conditions, tended to get smaller as governments tried to live within the orthodox doctrine of annually balanced budgets.

Keynes' approach led to the position that only through artificially induced higher levels of aggregate demand would it be possible to attain full employment and full utilization of plants and equipment. The course was clear: Business investment had to be stimulated, government spending had to be inflated, or, more likely, some combination of both had to be tried. The combined effects of expansionary fiscal policy (enlarged government spending and/or tax cuts usually accompanied by a budget deficit) and expansionary monetary policy (lower interest rates and easier money) were to produce enlarged aggregate demand and diminished unemployment.

THE VICTORY OF THE NEW ECONOMICS

Although Keynes quickly gained academic adherents for his ideas, he made little headway in Washington during the Depression. For all his alleged fiscal profligacy, Franklin Roosevelt, with his "pump priming" and "ABC" government agencies, never grasped the Keynesian analysis and never embraced massive federal spending until he was forced to—during World War II.

There was enormous federal spending during the war (with government spending in 1944 nearly twice the GNP of 1933), and this produced a rapid growth of demand that was restrained only by rationing and price controls. Simultaneously, there was an equally rapid growth in the federal debt. When the war ended, many economists still feared the economy would drop back into depression. Instead, the stored-up wartime demand became the engine for a long postwar boom. Even before the inadvertent Keynesianism of World War II proved to be effective, however, the United States had rung down the curtain on the laissez-faire era. On February 20, 1946, President Truman signed Public Law 340, better known as the Employment Act of 1946. The act committed the federal government to the three objectives of providing high levels of employment, maintaining stable prices, and encouraging economic growth. The groundwork had been laid for countercyclical fiscal and monetary policy.

The lessons of World War II fiscal expansion and the license for government fiscal and monetary intervention in the economy granted by the Employment Act of 1946 opened American economic thinking to the New Economics. Although Presidents Truman and Eisenhower showed only passing interest in the new doctrines and the new possibilities for public policy, the university economists were quickly won over.

With the election of John Kennedy in 1960, Keynesian theory became policy. Coming to office during the third Eisenhower recession (1960–1961), Kennedy introduced a fiscally experimental program. With an investment tax credit worth $2.5 billion to business in 1962 and the proposal for an $11 billion general tax cut in 1963, the Kennedy program offered sound Keynesian medicine. Lyndon Johnson continued and elaborated upon the Kennedy theme. For almost eight years the economy moved forward, and Americans learned (although they were soon to forget) that economic crisis, periodic or congenital, need not be the nature of the economy.

IS THE KEYNESIAN ANALYSIS STILL RELEVANT?

Since the late 1960s the ''New Economics'' has suffered badly in the press and at the hands of a resurgent laissez-faire element within the profession. Nor have Liberals been altogether confident about their Keynesian roots. Displaying a propensity ''to throw out the baby with the bath water,'' many economists, politicians, and ordinary citizens have incorrectly identified the Keynesian contribution as a primary cause of current macroeconomic problems. We shall return to this matter in the next issue on stabilization policy, but it is necessary to point out here that this is an unfair and inaccurate assessment of the contribution of the New Economics. It must be remembered that during the last two years of the 1960s and for most of the 1970s, Keynesian policy makers were effectively out of office in Washington. During this time, fiscal and monetary policy devices and objectives were subordinated to political opportunism and political needs or were simply handled in a stupid fashion.

The events of the 1970s also pointed out certain limitations of a too narrow Keynesian thinking. Keynes had focused his attention on an underemployed economy and on the means to counter depression. Keynes' followers had extended the antislump analysis to nonslump situations. Simply turning off the demand spigot through tight fiscal and monetary policies was viewed by many as sufficient for dealing with inflation, and alternatively turning on or off the spigot could amount to ''fine-tuning'' the economy so that there were neither slumps nor inflation. As we were to find out, it was too seductively simple; an economy undergoing the wrenching structural shocks of the 1970s (war, energy shortage, technological change, and the like) was not very responsive to ''fine-tuning'' efforts.

The Conservative allegations that it was Keynesianism that had pumped up the federal deficit (never mind the enormous cost of the Vietnam War or the political fiscal policy of the Johnson and Nixon years) and that the deficit had generated spiraling inflation (never mind the OPEC oil price increases) even gained some adherents among former Keynesians. Suddenly, some Liberals were agreeing with Conservatives that the federal deficit was the source of our economic problems and were advocating budget balance as the primary goal of fiscal policy. Conservatives, of course, wanted to go a step further, calling for a balanced budget amendment that would require as a matter of constitutional law that federal expenditures be limited to the amount of revenues collected. Most Liberals, however, recognize that if adopted, such an amendment would effectively destroy anti-depressionary fiscal policy. Budget limitations would make it impossible to use deficit spending as a device to enlarge aggregate demand. The nation would be returned to the vulnerability that existed in 1929, but this time it would be law rather than obsolete ideas that would inhibit countercyclical public policy. We shall expand on this point and recent political efforts to mandate a balanced budget in Issue 3.*

Although the Conservative attacks upon Keynesian logic and upon an activist fiscal and monetary policy remain a distinct threat to the nation's well-being, Liberals may find some comfort in irony. Ronald Reagan, articulator of a balanced-budget, Conservative macro policy, has in fact presided over the greatest expansion of the federal deficit in American history. Even Reagan's supply-side policies looked very much like traditional Keynesian efforts to stimulate the economy. His 1981 tax cut had precisely the save effect in pumping up demand as had Kennedy's in 1962. Indeed, if fiscal expansionism and budget deficits were the measure of "Keynesian" policy making, Conservative Reagan was the best Keynesian president yet.

The significance of this irony should not be overlooked. While Conservatives would heap all the blame for stagflation on misguided Keynesians, they do not admit that the "good" Reagan years rested on the same evils. We shall return to this point in detail in the next issue. Suffice to say here that they cannot have it both ways. The fact is that the economy, if it is not to slump off into recession or worse, depends on the periodic introduction of an expansionary fiscal and budget policy.

Is another Great Depression possible, then? Only, it would seem, if we forget the past and dismantle the public policy instruments we have created.

The Radical Argument

For both Conservatives and Liberals, albeit for different reasons, the imminent or future collapse of the American economy is not an inevitable event. Their views, of course, are not very startling. That

*In March 1986, the Senate failed to pass a balanced budget amendment by just one vote. Four months earlier, Congress had passed Gramm-Rudman-Hollings, which, in steps, established spending limits supposed to lead to a balanced budget by 1991. This bill was generally considered a silly undertaking, even by Conservative economists. Both its legality and its credibility remain in question at this writing. Nevertheless, we shall look at the act in detail in Issue 3.

defenders of varieties of capitalism believe the system has a future should be expected; however, the evidence, if looked at closely, points to a different conclusion. Contrary to the cheery Conservative view that free enterprise economies suffer only periodic and inconsequential business downturns, it is apparent from a historical as well as a recent perspective that crisis is part of the nature of production-for-profit economies. The Liberal contention that the countercyclical use of fiscal and monetary policy can insulate us from depression enormously understates the systemic roots of economic crisis and fails to comprehend the costs and effects of the tools of countercyclical policy.

THE CHRONIC TENDENCY TOWARD CRISIS

Economic crisis and instability are not peculiar to capitalist societies alone. However, with the dawn and maturity of capitalism, crisis (or what we presently might call depression) took on a new dimension. In precapitalist societies, economic contraction resulted largely from wars, plagues, crop failures, or other natural disasters. The granaries were empty, people starved, and there were shortages of goods of all kinds. Crisis was associated with underproduction. Paradoxically, in the capitalist era of crisis, this situation has been reversed. Capitalist contraction usually appears after an era of growth in the productive forces of a society. With excess goods on hand and no market, producers reduce current output, unemployment rises, and wages and prices fall. In short, capitalist crises usually begin when the granaries are full.

To be sure, the periodic panics and depressions that strike capitalism have usually been followed by recoveries. For many years, before the appearance of Keynes' work, the periodicity of boom and bust (especially boom) allowed Conservatives to describe economic contractions as "mere disturbances" that would go away and therefore did not merit very serious analytical study. No effort was made to see stagnation as fundamental to the capitalist order. Nor has this view changed much among modern Conservative economists. Keynesian Liberals, meanwhile, have accepted the fact that underconsumption generally leads to depressions in modern capitalism, but they hold that the tendency is easily manageable through the tools of modern public policy.

From the Radical perspective, however, economic crises are both fundamental to capitalism and beyond the capitalists' capacity to resolve. As capitalist economies grow and mature, crises become ever more frequent and progressively deeper, each succeeded by a less satisfactory recovery.

The crises are inherent in the capitalist system of production. In their perpetual search for expanded profits, capitalists must create surplus value—that is, they forever attempt to maximize the difference between the higher price for which goods sell and the lower price of the labor involved in production. To acquire greater profits, the capitalist must enlarge surplus value through the introduction of greater amounts of capital equipment, through the direct exploitation of labor, or through some combination of the two. The object is to produce greater output per unit of wage labor paid. As capitalists endeavor to produce more and more at greater profit, the capacity of the workers (consumers) to purchase this output declines. Although the people may ''need'' the goods, they do not have the ''effective demand'' to obtain them. Overproduction and underconsumption create periodic gluts of goods, which in turn cause crises wherein production ceases, capital is destroyed or left idle, and human beings starve.

As capitalism progresses, its productive capacity constantly enlarges. The possible depths and duration of production-consumption crises are heightened, and the ultimate end of the system is brought that much closer. Nineteenth-century Marxists observed the growing incidence of capitalist crises and predicted early collapse as profits fell, unemployment grew, real wages declined, and the system became discredited before the masses.

In point of fact, all this has not happened, but that is not proof that the underlying Radical analysis was wrong. Rather, it must be adjusted to take certain events into account.

First, the capitalists' persistent need for markets to dispose of their surplus production and to realize surplus value and profits was partially attained through overseas exploitation—imperialism. One case might illustrate the point. In the latter half of the nineteenth century, the depressed British textile industry experienced a significant boom after the British colonial rulers of India systematically destroyed the Indian weaving industry. British machines, and even British workers, went back to work precisely as Indians were forced from old occupations and compelled to buy imported British textiles.

Second, capitalist enterprise, which Marx had depicted as largely competitive, began to respond to the periodic crises by developing monopolistic characteristics. Industries became more integrated and dominated by a few firms. Possessing the power to set and control prices, output, and quality, monopoly capitalism was able to avoid the internecine struggles that had wiped out enterprises in the earlier competitive era.

Third, the growth of the state in the economy provided additional insulation from crisis. The state could foster or sanction monopoly behavior, mitigate the effects of labor exploitation and unemployment, and act directly to absorb the surplus production through government purchases (especially during war) and transfer payments.

THE COLLAPSE OF 1929

The expansion of overseas markets and sources of cheap labor and resources, the increasingly monopolistic behavior of business enterprises, and the enlargement of government protective actions held back the breaking of the dike before 1929. It did not, however, stop serious leaks.

In the case of the United States, seven major business cycles can be identified between the panic of 1893 and the beginning of World War I. Each downturn lasted longer and became more pronounced. As the United States entered World War I and a wartime business boom, unemployment stood at about 10 percent. The "roaring twenties" were not much better. Probably the worst depression in U.S. history to that point occurred in 1921–1922, and throughout most of the decade unemployment was higher than 4 percent. Meanwhile, real wages moved upward only slightly. Only the phenomenal expansion of consumer debt buoyed the economy. For those who wished to see the evidence or could at least understand it, it was apparent that the dike would soon collapse.

The crisis after 1929 was a near-classic example of Marx's overproduction-underconsumption scenario. Moreover, it precipitated a general international collapse. The mature capitalist economies had exhausted markets for their goods. Overseas, the underdeveloped economies had little capacity to absorb output. At home, warehouses bulged since consumers lacked effective demand. As the first signs of crisis appeared, the banking and financial system, which itself rested upon the capitalists' ability to realize their surplus, tottered and collapsed: first the Wall Street crash, then New York bank failures, then European bank failures. Full-scale industrial contraction followed.

THE OLD ECONOMICS IN A NEW PACKAGE

The Keynesian response to the deepening Depression was to accept the essential outline of the older Marxist critique of capitalism: Overproduction and crisis were endemic to the system. However, the Keynesians neatly evaded the Marxian conclusion. According to their analysis, insufficient business and consumer demand could be either manipulated by fiscal and monetary policy or supplemented by government spending so as to raise the level of aggregate demand. In Marxian terms, government now became the vehicle to "realize surplus value."

Much has been made of this new thinking on the problem of the capitalist system. The "Keynesian Revolution" came to describe dominant economic opinion; however, it was no revolution at all. Keynes and his followers have not sought to end capitalism but to save it. The central features of capitalism—private property, production for profit, wage labor, the business system, and all the rest— were retained. Indeed, as business leaders came to appreciate the profit (surplus value) possibilities of enlarged government spending during World War II and the trial-and-error Keynesian years after the war, corporate America enthusiastically accepted the new economics. The frequent Liberal posturing against big business should be recognized as pure political rhetoric. In the 1964 Johnson-Goldwater electoral contest, big business showed its colors by rejecting the Conservative, laissez-faire Republican in favor of the big-spending Democrat from Texas. Giant corporations poured millions of dollars into LBJ's campaign.

THE KEYNESIAN MIRAGE AND BACK TO REALITY

Through the 1960s and most of the 1970s (remember that even Richard Nixon had proclaimed himself a Keynesian), the New Economics seemed to be just what capitalism needed. The old capitalist business cycle of roller-coaster ups and downs simply disappeared as the economy underwent continuous expansion. In silly self-congratulation, economists wrote and talked of "no more depressions" while they enjoyed a place never before reserved for them in the public's esteem.

With the Vietnam War and other government spending growing and an easy monetary policy usually operating to encourage private borrowing, high levels of demand kept factories operating at near-peak utilization rates and kept unemployment rates low. Yet these signs of success through the 1960s were in fact danger signals, for in capitalism success invariably sows the seeds of doom. The basic problem, as with all expansionary phases of the capitalist business cycle, was that expanding demand put serious pressures on business by causing rising costs, which in turn squeezed profits. With unemployment at very low levels, workers, unionized and nonunionized alike, enjoyed a seller's market for their labor. Real wages rose as businesses bid against each other for needed employees. Between 1960 and 1973, real (adjusted for inflation) after-tax weekly earnings rose by 35 percent. Since this exceeded productivity (output per worker-hour) growth, it translated into rising per-unit costs for producers. To make matters worse, resource costs worldwide began rising, the principal source being rising energy costs resulting from the Arabs' opting to challenge their former colonial and neocolonial masters.

At any rate, after-tax corporate profits peaked in 1965 (at about 10.5 percent on investment) and fell thereafter (to about 4.5 percent in 1974). With profits falling, businesses continued to reduce their investment outlays through the late 1960s and into the 1970s. At first the decline was scarcely felt as demand remained high for a time, but in the late 1960s, unemployment began to edge upward. By the early 1970s, regardless of expansionary fiscal policy efforts to offset the trend, unemployment grew as profits fell. Prices, meanwhile, began to rise, producing the new phenomenon of *stagflation* (rising unemployment *and* rising prices). Inflation took hold simply because demand, fueled by government and private borrowing, remained high. Without an expansion of busines production facilities and with productive efficiency falling as the investment base got older and more outmoded, the high levels of demand caused price increases rather than output expansion. Meanwhile, the high levels of demand had few salutary effects on employment since profits remained low and business actually reduced its rate of investment. The outer limits of runaway Keynesianism had been reached.

There remained only one solution—the old solution: recession. Through the mid- and late 1970s, under enormous pressure from rising prices, government fiscal policy turned less expansionary. Predictably, unemployment crept upward. Inflation, however, was not significantly slowed until Conservative Ronald Reagan slew the dragon with a bone-chilling tight money policy that shut off private borrowing. The immediate result was the recession of 1981–1983, which produced Great Depression levels of unemployment.

Although the new supply-side Conservatives crowed about their victory over inflation and enjoyed pointing out that Keynesianism had proved itself a failure, they, as we shall see in the next issue, understood little about what had happened. They offered no new "solution" to the capitalist system. However, the growing popularity of Conservative antigovernment, probusiness thinking, in the wake of the retreat from Keynes, was profoundly ironic. Marx, commenting on the ironies of history, once remarked that when history repeats itself, it first appears as tragedy and then as farce. However, to the more thoughtful, the idea of America returning to the "good old days" of Calvin Coolidge and Herbert Hoover is both farcical *and* tragic.

Yet, in a sense, that is precisely where we are. Indeed, production-for-profit capitalism, in any substantial sense, has never really passed much beyond the era immediately preceding the Great Depression. Is another Great Depression possible? *Very definitely*.

ISSUE 2

Stabilization and Growth Policy for the 1980s and Beyond
Supply Side or Demand Side?

We must recognize that only experience can show how far the common will, embodied in the policy of the state, ought to be directed to increasing and supplementing the inducement to invest.

John Maynard Keynes, 1935

Is fiscal policy being oversold? Is monetary policy being oversold? . . . My answer is yes to both of those questions. . . . What I believe is that fine tuning has been oversold.

Milton Friedman, 1968

The potency of fiscal policy—both good and bad—has been demonstrated time and again in the past couple of decades.

Walter W. Heller, 1968

Originating in a liberal effort to respond to the popular will and relieve the pressures of poverty, demand-oriented politics ends in promoting unemployment and dependency.

George Gilder, 1981

Was the new [supply side] approach successful in raising productivity and bringing down inflation at little cost? While the verdict is not in, there is evidently no sea-change in the United States since 1980.

Paul Samuelson, 1985

THE PROBLEM

As we saw in the last issue, Conservative, Liberal, and Radical paradigms are strikingly divided on the matter of long-run economic stability within a capitalist economy and on the macroeconomic role to be played by government within an essentially production-for-profit system. While these larger and more spectacular questions of whether or not the economy is ultimately depression-proof always loom in the background, the problems of short-run economic performance attract greater attention from economists and public officials. In other words, more day-to-day concern is placed upon the trim of the economic ship than upon what might be done if it actually capsized. Obviously the two concerns are not unrelated; however, we shall look more closely at specific policy measures aimed at maintaining our short-run economic stability and growth.

Since the passage of the Employment Act of 1946, the federal government has had the responsibility

> to use all practicable means consistent with its needs and obligations and other essential considerations of national policy, with assistance and co-operation of industry, agriculture, labor and State and local governments, to coordinate and utilize all its plans, functions, and resources for the purpose of creating and maintaining, in a manner calculated to foster and promote free competitive enterprise and general welfare, conditions under which there will be afforded useful employment opportunities, including self-employment, for those able, willing and seeking to work and to promote maximum employment, production and purchasing power.

This careful and legal jargon has been simplified over the years to three basic public policy objectives: providing high levels of employment, maintaining stable prices, and encouraging economic growth. Although presidential comprehension of and adherence to the public policy objectives of the act have varied with intellect and ideology since 1946, these goals have, for most mainstream economists, been the essence of government economic policy for the past four decades. They are the great trinity of modern macro policy thought and analysis.

As we have seen earlier, the New Economics of John Maynard Keynes, with its emphasis on demand-side management, emerged as the dominant doctrine by the 1960s. The basic strategy of demand managers was to "fine-tune" the economy by controlling the spigot of aggregate demand. The *Economic Report of the President* in 1965 put it this way: "Fiscal and monetary policies must be continually adjusted to keep the aggregate demand for goods and services in line with the economy's growing capacity to produce them." In the 1970s and early 1980s, however, everything turned to ashes for the Keynesians. "Stagflation" became a chronic condition, and it caused great agonizing among economists and politicians as to how to end the episode and return to a stable and growing economy. The economy slumped through four major recessions in less than a dozen years. But even in nonrecessionary years, unemployment remained chronically high. Moreover, inflation persisted in both good years and bad. Most important, though, was the performance of the economy's growth rate, the average annual increase in gross national product (the value of a year's output of goods and services). From a rate of nearly 4.5 percent a year during the prosperous 1960s, the rate fell to under 2 percent at the beginning of the 1980s.

The demand managers seemed immobilized in the face of these developments, but a new breed of conservative "supply-siders" were eager to take up the new problems.* Their arguments ran like this: Stimulation of aggregate demand only produces effects on output and employment when an economy has sunk into very low levels of production (in other words, 1930s-style depression). Under the more usual conditions of the 1970s and 1980s, efforts to expand the economy by increasing demand primarily had the effect of raising prices.†

Price increases in turn push up interest rates and have a negative effect on business investment decisions. A more intelligent strategy, according to supply-siders, would be to increase the nation's productive capacity, focusing therefore on factors that increase supply rather than demand. Increases in the productive base and in the productivity of the private sector, not government-stimulated demand, were to make growth without inflation possible.

With the Conservative Ronald Reagan coming to the White House in 1981, Conservatives finally got a crack at "solving" the modern macroeconomic crisis. While Liberals argued that the supply-siders were re-

*Among the better-known of this group were economists Paul Craig Roberts, Norman Ture, and Arthur Laffer and economics writer Jude Winniski.

†This point can be demonstrated fairly simply in the aggregate demand and aggregate supply graphs on p. 56. With aggregate demand (AD) and aggregate supply (AS) respectively illustrating the total demand and total supply of goods at all possible combinations of GNP and price level, the economy is in equilibrium in panel 1, where AD = AS. It

ally just returning to the old doctrine of giving businesses greater economic freedom in their production activities (a step backward from a Liberal perspective), the supply-siders won some quick and impressive political victories. The Revenue Reform Act of 1981 brought a three-year, 25 percent reduction in personal taxes and a substantial reduction in business taxes. Flushed with victory, the Conservatives proceeded to take a meat cleaver to the budget they had inherited from the Liberal democrats.

As of this writing, supply-side efforts in chopping federal expenditures have been a lot less impressive than their tax-reduction efforts. As a result, Conservative Reagan became the author of the largest deficits in American history. Defenders, however, could point to the fact that by late 1983, the economy had begun to rebound and continued to do so through 1986—and the rebound came about as inflation rates fell to one-third or less of their late-1970s levels. On the other hand, Liberals argued, there had been no marvelous increase in productivity, and unemployment remained high by past prosperity standards. The jury was still

---

can be noted that at a low level of equilibrium output (Q), an increase in total demand from AD to AD_1 has a far greater impact in increasing GNP than in raising the price level. However, the shift from AD_1 to AD_2 has a far greater impact on prices. The reason is obvious: As the aggregate supply curve approaches full employment, it slopes upward more swiftly, since increased competition among buyers of increasingly scarce resources bids up prices. The solution to the problem is demonstrated in panel 2. Actions should be taken that shift AS (increase aggregate supply) to the right. This will facilitate, *ceteris paribus*, an increase in GNP and a decrease in prices.

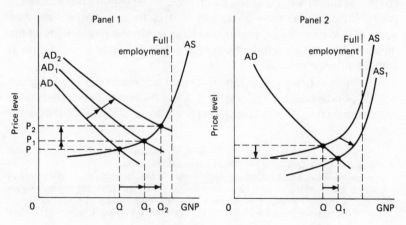

out on the real contribution of supply-side economics, and many believed it was still out on the question of whether or not demand-side efforts had in fact been the failure Conservatives alleged.

SYNOPSIS. Conservatives argue that past efforts at stabilization policy have not only failed to fine-tune the economy but have also been instrumental in creating our present economic stagnation. They argue instead for an approach to stabilization and growth that emphasizes tax and spending reductions and balancing the federal budget. Liberals interpret the stabilization record of the past quite differently, pointing out that "random shocks" over which economists had little or no control were the primary cause for the current stagflation epoch. They still argue on behalf of an active fiscal policy in bringing and keeping the economy under control. Radicals see the past efforts of Liberal stabilization policy as an effort to intervene in the economy on behalf of business and ruling-class interests. The recent attempts to dismantle the old stabilization policies are a passing aberration, a measure of capitalism's modern crisis.

Anticipating the Arguments

- What are the basic components of a supply-side economic policy?

- In the face of recent economic difficulties, how do Liberals defend demand management?

- On what grounds do Radicals reject both supply-side and demand-side approaches?

The Conservative Argument

Having incorrectly assumed that massive injections of government spending were the cures to any drastic economic downturn, Liberal Keynesians have elaborated equally spurious doctrines about fine-tuning the economy in "normal" times. According to their view, expansionary monetary and fiscal policy could effectively offset minor but troublesome downturns in output and employment. Conversely, contractionary actions could lessen inflationary pressures. The public policy spigot need only be adjusted to produce the desired flow. This idea has been one of the most dangerous frauds ever perpetrated upon a free people, and it demands to be exposed. In fact, demand management has produced a roller-coaster effect— one economic cycle after another of fighting unemployment with inflationary public policy followed by fighting inflation with unemployment.

THE NEED FOR A NEW DIRECTION

Americans were oversold on the possibilities of a better life through fiscal expansionism. ''Fine tuning'' simply never got beyond Liberal economists' lecture notes. The record speaks for itself. Since the 1960s, Keynesian fiscal policy has been synonymous with rising federal expenditures and a growing mountain of federal debt. Federal spending grew by almost 600 percent between 1960 and 1980, and debt increased by more than 300 percent. While Liberals argued that such expansionism was necessary to maintain a full-employment economy, Figure 2.1 shows that unemployment actually worsened over these years. Meanwhile, the excessive growth of government debt pumped up the money supply, triggering a long inflationary spiral (see Issue 3).

With the Keynesian heresy exposed as a failure, it is time for a

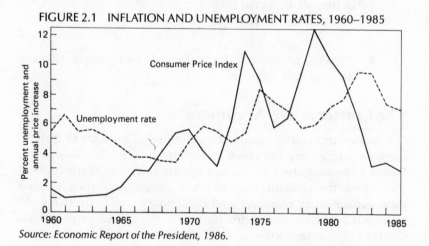

FIGURE 2.1   INFLATION AND UNEMPLOYMENT RATES, 1960–1985

Source: Economic Report of the President, 1986.

new approach. The Conservative program for stabilization and growth requires going back and reassessing what we knew before Keynes and adding what we have learned since Keynes. It is composed of three basic elements: (1) Redirect fiscal and monetary policy attention from the demand or consumption side of economic activity to the supply or production side, (2) oppose public policy actions that would return us to the awful demand inflation of the Keynesian years, and (3) restrain the disruptive effects of government spending by developing and maintaining a balanced federal budget. In this issue, we shall concentrate on the benefits obtained from a stabilization policy aimed at the supply side; in the next, we will look at the destructive impact of Liberal demand-side efforts that produce inflation and persistent federal deficits.

To a limited extent, some of the Conservative agenda has been implemented during the Reagan years, particularly the part aimed at redirecting attention to the supply side. Based on the evidence so far, it has done what it was supposed to do. The economy pulled out of its decade of troubles in 1983, posting a more than 7 percent annual growth rate in 1984, the biggest real growth in more than a decade. Moreover, as Figure 2.1 indicates, both inflation and unemployment rates fell from 1982 to 1985. Such gains, however, are only a beginning. Much more remains to be done.

PAYING ATTENTION TO THE SUPPLY SIDE

Until recently, conventional macroeconomics was taught only one-dimensionally. Following the Keynesian critique of an economy in deep depression, with great quantities of labor unemployed and much of the nation's plants and equipment sitting idle, majority economic reasoning saw the economic dilemma as simply a problem of inadequate demand: Increase the demand for goods, and men, women, and machines would go back to work. In such a view, the supply side was taken for granted. Whatever amount of output might be demanded—right up to the point at which people and machines were fully employed—would be supplied virtually instantaneously. End of the Keynesian story.

To see where the Keynesian critique errs and to understand how and why Liberal stabilization policy goes awry, we must digress briefly to clear up a couple of analytical points. The object is to establish that aggregate supply cannot be assumed to be an unimportant and neutral variable in any realistic discussion of how the aggregate economy works.

First of all, the aggregate supply of goods reflects cost considerations. Perhaps adding additional workers or using previously idled production facilities in deeply recessionary or depressionary general economic conditions has little effect on unit production costs. However, that is not the case when an economy approaches full employment. In fact, well before full employment is encountered, production costs may be rising. Additional workers and raw materials are, after all, obtained in competition with other firms seeking workers and materials; wages and prices are accordingly bid upwards. In other words, while output may in fact be increased in response to an increase in demand all the way up to full employment levels, after some point, usually well short of full employment, output increases reflect greatly increasing production costs and rising prices. Thus the impact of increasing the demand for goods may be mostly to raise prices rather than to increase output. Given this theoretical situation, we can begin to see some of the problems demand-side managers were encountering in the 1960s and 1970s. Expansionary fiscal and monetary policy efforts were bumping up against rising supply costs, with the result that prices were going up and few increases in real output were obtained. And as we shall see later, the inflationary pressures were counterproductive—lowering real output and creating more unemployment. We had encountered stagflation.

The second point to note about aggregate supply is that it reflects the existing productive base of an economy. The more efficient and productive a society is, the lower the unit production costs are and the less likely they are to rise for any given increase in demand. Through the 1960s and 1970s, the productive base of the American economy was allowed to weaken as public policy concentrated only on the demand side.

Before the ascendancy of Keynesian ideas, conventional economic wisdom held that "supply creates its own demand." The emphasis of economic doctrine and policy was on the supply side. Quite inaccurately, and with disastrous results, the old wisdom became rewritten to read: "Demand creates its own supply." Nothing could be further from the truth.

THE SUPPLY SIDE "MENU"

By shifting our attention over the past fifty years from basic problems of production to the demand side of the market, we have shackled the basic productive structure of the economy and weakened our own capacity to produce. Once the model of industrial output, productivity by American workers and industry is near the bottom among industrial nations, and the trend can be broken only by developing new supply-side growth policies.

First, *savings must be encouraged*. Modern Keynesians incorrectly view savings as a reduction of total demand. However, without savings, funds are not available for the business investment required to reinvigorate American industry and make it once again competitive with foreign producers. Tired and old capital equipment and procedures are basic causes of our current inefficiency. Over the past several decades, our tax policies, with heavy progressive taxes on upper-income groups (who are most likely to be the savers) and our high corporate profits taxes, have diminished our investment potential. Though called income taxes, these revenues have really been "savings taxes." As Arthur Laffer has pointed out, the irony of our tax approach in the past is that higher tax rates have the effect of producing lower tax collections. As work and savings incentives are lowered by rising rates, there is less output to tax. Thus lower tax rates, not higher ones, should produce more output and, ironically, more tax revenues.

The supply-sider objective of enhancing savings was implemented into policy during the Reagan years. The reduction of taxes on capital gains and the personal income tax reductions in the 1981 Revenue Reform Act were significant victories. Similarly the reductions of taxes on saved income, through tax-sheltered IRA accounts introduced in 1981, are a powerful potential incentive for saving. As of this writing, Congress is considering a presidential proposal that will lower effective tax rates still further. Although some tax deductions will be lost in such a reform, many of these deductions have actually acted to encourage consumption rather than savings (for example, being able to deduct interest charges on second home mortgages and consumer credit from taxable income).

Second, *the "tax wedge" must be reduced*. Apart from the disincentives of high tax rates on savings and corporate profits, taxes also have the effect of creating a "cost-push" effect on prices. That is, rising sales, excise, payroll, and other corporate taxes become added onto the final prices of goods. With taxes raising the relative price of goods, total demand for goods falls. This in turn reduces corporate sales and induces layoffs and plant closings. Holding down various business taxes, including corporate income taxes which may in part be pushed forward as part of a firm's costs, are a virtual necessity.

Third, *restrictions on business investment and risk taking must be reduced*. New business undertakings, both in producing new goods and in producing old goods in new ways, will expand national employment and national economic growth faster than any other approach. Yet a maze of government regulations over marketing and production activities hampers business enterprise. As a result, business adjusts downward to lower levels of output and lagging growth performance. To stimulate risk taking, we must reduce the regulatory overkill that exists in our economy. The Liberal "interventions" in consumer, environmental, and job safety areas are not free. They raise business costs just as the tax wedge does, and the results are rising prices, rising unemployment, and plant closings.

Fourth, *greater labor force participation and mobility should be encouraged*. Liberals have not faced up to the realities of American labor markets. Expensive welfare programs, which account for the bulk of federal spending growth since the 1960s, have been designed to cushion the effects of unemployment. In fact, they have nurtured unemployment. With lavish benefits for not working, there is little economic incentive for workers to improve skills, to relocate where jobs do exist, or to view work itself in a positive way. Transfers of funds to the unemployed may pump up their spending, but these increases in aggregate demand are more than offset by supply reductions resulting from a combination of high wages (to induce workers to work) and high taxes (to support workers who won't work).

SUPPLY-SIDE IMPACT OF DEFICITS AND INFLATION

Although we shall examine the destabilizing effects of federal deficits and excess demand inflation in some detail in the next issue, their specific impact on the supply side of economic activity must be underlined here.

Not only does inflation gnaw at purchasing power and lower real demand, but it also interferes with business investment decisions, foreign trade, and financial and securities markets. The results are lowered business expectations and production levels that throw millions of people out of work. No one has ever argued the case that unemployment causes inflation; usually it is assumed to have some depressing effect upon prices. But evidence from all the great inflationary spirals of the past shows that inflation *does* eventually depress employment. Meanwhile, a minimal mastery of macroeconomics should permit us to see that any public policy efforts to heat up the economy for the purpose of creating jobs can only add to existing inflationary pressures.

Some will say that this is a hardhearted position. They will argue that Conservatives care little about people who are unemployed. That is not true. Solving the inflation problem is a Conservative answer to the unemployment problem. A privately oriented economy with low interest rates, reasonably assured business expectations, and a slow but steady rate of money expansion to support higher levels of demand will be a growing economy. That means more jobs. An economic system dominated by government, where either monetary policy or fiscal policy (or both) is used recklessly to create jobs, will limit the freedom of the private sector, interfere with the business investment, and sooner or later worsen the unemployment problem.

Meanwhile, government deficits, usually the cause of inflationary pressures and always the effect of imprudent fiscal policies, get in their whacks at the supply side. Government debt tends to *crowd out* private investment activities; that is, private borrowers are squeezed out of investment fund markets when government borrows large quantities of money at very high interest rates. As a result, the supposedly expansionary effects of government debts (as the Keynesians argue) are wholly offset by reductions in private borrowing. Far from having the impact of increasing total demand and hence growth and jobs, public debt causes offsetting or greater-than-offsetting private-sector reactions. The impact, however, is not entirely on the demand side. Investment not undertaken is also production facilities not added. The capacity to produce is diminished.

LOOKING TOWARD THE LONG RUN

Liberal critics of supply-side efforts, while grudgingly acknowledging a few gains in the leveling off of inflation and the decline of unemployment rates, point out that no "miracle" has swept the American economy. They fail to realize, however, that the supply-side focus is over the medium to long run. Quick, up-front paybacks from adopting supply-side policies were never promised. Even after the distortions of five decades of Liberal Keynesian mismanagement are overcome, time is needed for the production side of the economy to adjust to new economic conditions. The quick fix—indeed, one quick fix after another—was the hallmark of Liberal policy making. Conservative supply-oriented policies presuppose the gradual creation of market conditions that return economic order. Both pain and time are costs that must be incurred as we adjust to a new manner of economic thought.

The Liberal Argument

In the last issue, we laid out the case for fiscal and monetary policy to counter depressions. In brief, the argument held that since the Great Depression and the appearance of the Keynesian critique, we do possess adequate policy tools to manage the general level of economic activity. However, possessing the tools and using them correctly are different matters. In the case of fiscal policy, how effective have we really been and what should we presently be doing?

Conservatives, who do not believe in the efficacy of fiscal policy, are in fact long on theory and short on evidence. What evidence they do offer begs correct interpretation. Far from being "proven" ineffective in the past and the "cause" of present stagflation problems, fiscal management of the general level of economic activity had a good record during the 1960s. To understand the recent crisis of the macroeconomy, we need to look at a number of developments unconnected to the theory and practice of Keynesian stabilization policy. First, there was the outright misuse of countercyclical policy during most of the 1970s. More important, however, were the series of unpredictable random shocks that hit the economy during this period, along with certain subtle structural shifts within the economy.

THE FISCAL POLICY RECORD EXAMINED

The general framework of antidepressionary policy making was in place by the beginning of the post–World War II period. Steps to end the Depression, wartime spending, and the legal commitment of the Employment Act of 1946 helped to end the traditional government commitment to a balanced budget. Nevertheless, between 1946 and the early 1960s, the political leadership of the nation showed little mastery of the new policy possibilities. Fiscal policy, as it was practiced, was unplanned and ill-timed. Deficits or surpluses appeared at the wrong times or quite accidentally at the right time. Manipulative monetary policy was not practiced at all.

With John Kennedy's election in 1960, as we noted in the last issue, countercyclical fiscal policy was to get its chance. The Kennedy tax cuts of 1962–1963 and increased presidential awareness of how the aggregate economy could be manipulated by stabilizing fiscal and monetary policy meant the coming of the age of macro policy making. There followed several years of economic growth, falling unemployment rates, and steady prices—precisely what the Employment Act of 1946 called for and Keynesian economists promised they could deliver.

The experiment in stabilization, however, was to be short-lived. The expanded war in Vietnam, coupled with Johnson's adamant stance that the economy could produce guns *and* butter, began to pump up excess demand. Richard Nixon's continuation of the war after 1969 and his own timidity in dealing with growing excess demand brought the short era of stabilization policy to an end.

The failure of fiscal policy in the late 1960s, however, was not a defeat for theory. If Johnson had shared his war intentions with his economic advisors and also shown more political courage, a tax increase in 1966 or 1967 could have cooled the economy down. Nixon, too, failed to utilize the fiscal brakes, fearing political reaction to a tax increase. Instead he sought to deal with the inflationary push by instituting an ineffective program of wage and price controls and by having the monetary authorities put a squeeze on demand through tight money. When excess demand inflation should have been halted according to elementary Keynesian analysis, this was not done.

As a consequence of these political developments, we have only a comparatively short period, roughly from 1962 to 1969, to evaluate countercyclical fiscal policy. However, these years stand out boldly in attaining the objectives of the Employment Act of 1946. Table 2.1 compares three important indicators—changes in per capita income, unemployment levels, and the consumer price index—over the eight years of Keynesian ascendancy with comparable periods before and since. As the data indicate, per capita income growth and unemployment levels had their most desirable showing between 1962 and 1969, and only the recessed Eisenhower years posted a slower increase in the consumer price index. Alas, Camelot was all too brief, but it did provide proof of the effectiveness of modern fiscal policy management.

RANDOM SHOCKS AND STRUCTURAL CHANGES

Contrary to the Conservative view that Keynesian stabilization policy caused the general price increases of the 1970s and 1980s, the real cause was a series of random events that built an inflationary bias into the economy. In the period between 1971 and 1973, the Nixon administration attempted to devalue the dollar to ease worsening U.S. balance-of-payments problems (which were caused mostly by our Vietnam War spending). While U.S. goods were more attractive in foreign markets as a result of devaluation, foreign goods became expensive in the United States. *Result*: Domestic prices of

Table 2.1   Average Annual Changes in Per Capita Income, Average Annual Unemployment, and Average Annual Changes in the Consumer Price Index for Selected Periods

Year	Change in Real Per Capita Income (%)	Unemployment Rate	Change in Consumer Price Index (%)
1954–1961	1.6	5.4	1.1
1962–1969	3.1	4.5	2.4
1970–1977	2.0	6.3	8.2
1978–1985	2.1	7.6	7.4

Source: Economic Report of the President, 1986.

imported goods went up. In October 1973, the United States exported 19 million metric tons of wheat to the Soviet Union, reducing American supplies of grain to practically nothing. *Result*: Domestic food prices rose about 50 percent over the next four years. At about the same time, there was a growing world shortage of critical minerals and other raw materials. *Result*: Prices for finished goods went up. In late 1973, OPEC (Organization of Petroleum Exporting Countries) began a long series of petroleum price increases that raised crude oil charges from less than $2 per barrel to nearly $40 by 1981. *Result*: All prices were forced upward.

The effect of these inflationary shocks was to create an inflationary psychology in the nation. Each event seemed to support the view that prices would continue to go up. These "rational expectations" of future inflation induced both labor unions and businesses to act to protect themselves from future inflationary shocks. Wages and prices began to go up even faster than the rise caused by the random inflationary events. The effect of this general inflationary increase, which saw the consumer price index more than double between 1970 and 1980, was to lower consumers' real buying power. The inflation "tax" reduced the spendable income of ordinary consumers and businesses, and aggregate demand fell. With falling demand and slowing economic growth, there was an accompanying rise in unemployment.

Clearly the situation called for capping inflationary increases by some use of price controls while maintaining employment and growth through appropriate fiscal policy. This was not to be the case. President Carter's first efforts in 1978 and 1979 at voluntary wage-price guidelines were a complete failure. At the same time, expansionary efforts to reduce unemployment were blocked by Conservatives who decided that inflation was the biggest problem and who wrongly concluded that inflation was the result of past fiscal policy excesses.

EVALUATING THE SUPPLY-SIDE ARGUMENT

Despite the initially innovative appearance of Conservative supply-side theory, time has shown that its originality is negligible and its effectiveness marginal. To be sure, the rampant inflation of the late 1970s slowed down, but this was not the demonstrated result of supply-side policies or new economic thinking of any kind. Pursuing a tight-money, high-interest-rate monetary policy, the Conservative Reagan administration succeeded in applying what everyone had always known was a possible cure to inflation: *They created a deep recession in 1982–1983.* Construction, business investment, and new factory orders came to a standstill, and unemployment rose to Great Depression levels. To no one's surprise, prices fell—not because of any action on the supply side but simply because demand dried up.

The economy did begin to improve, however, in late 1983, and a miniboom continued beyond 1985. Was this perhaps the effect of supply-side policy? Supply-siders point to the 25 percent personal income tax reduction (over three years) and a variety of "enhancements" in business taxes enacted in 1981 as the source of economic improvement. There is not much doubt that the tax cuts did stimulate a boom, but the tax cuts had their effect from the demand side, not the supply side. Consumer spending went up, but changes in business investment were scarcely noticeable. Moreover, the boom was greatly inspired by vast increases in government spending for military goods and an exploding federal deficit. What the supply-siders were calling a victory looked exactly like the defeats they alleged to a demand-oriented policy.

To be sure, prices increased only very slowly during the mid-1980s. Was this necessary evidence that a supply-side focus to stabilization policy worked? In fact, prices were low for a number of other reasons. First, the very depth of the 1982 recession meant that the economy could climb upward without exerting many price pressures. Second, world energy prices fell during this period. Third, a world economic slump followed our recession and also tended to have a downward effect on prices. Fourth, a strengthening American dollar (see Issue 7) invited a flood of foreign competition into American markets, holding down domestic price increases.

The sought-after increase in savings that was supposed to provide the source of new investment never materialized. In fact, savings rates of Americans went down, not up, after the 1981 tax cut. Meanwhile, real harm resulted from other supply-side programs. Unemployment remained high, falling only 3 percent to 7 percent between 1982 and 1986. At the same time, low-income Americans suffered as Conservatives chiseled away at social welfare programs that were singled out as both the cause of federal deficits and a troublesome source of "stickiness" in labor markets. The persistent unemployment, the healthy tax cuts for the well-to-do and for business, and the dismantling of much of the social safety net that supported lower-income citizens had not brought a new opportunity for most Americans. Instead, the gap was widened between those at the top and those at the bottom of the economic ladder.

Supply-side stabilization policy stands revealed as either a very "meanhearted" policy or no policy at all. The crowning objective of the supply-siders, the constitutional enforcement of a balanced federal budget, will absorb our attention in the next issue. Suffice it for now to point out that legally required budget balance would make supply-side policy even meaner since social programs would be sacrificed to obtain balance: Ultimately, with tax increases off limits as a balancing alternative and military spending a "sacred cow," only social spending is left as the balancing item. However, an even bigger problem develops because budget balance means the effective end of any activist fiscal policy. The result would be to leave the nation disarmed in any war with short-term business cycle changes.

Supply-side Conservatives are correct, and Liberals have never really disputed the point, that a nation's productive base is the ultimate determinant of its capacity to produce. However, the condition of a nation's production facilities is not the only factor determining output. The level of demand also plays its role. By focusing on the supply side, Conservatives show understanding of only half the economic problem. And half a solution is really no solution at all.

FISCAL POLICY AND BEYOND

From the foregoing argument, the Liberal position should be clear: First, the fiscal tools of government taxing and spending are useful devices by which we can manage the general performance of the economy, whether it be dealing with inflation or unemployment. Second, although assigned a lesser role, monetary policy should be coordinated with and "lean" in the same direction as fiscal policy. Third, fiscal and monetary policies should be developed so as to have desirable and humane social effects, spreading the tax burden and the spending so as to close the economic gap between those at the bottom and those at the top of the economic ladder. Finally, unemployment should always be seen as the most important economic problem, and it must receive our attention in fiscal policy making *first*. Any other approach will tear the fabric of our society. Faced with the problem of the Great Depression, Herbert Hoover, a president deeply committed to a Conservative fiscal outlook, once lectured a visiting delegation of mayors on the evils of deficits and enlarged government spending. "Gentlemen," he asked, "can you think of anything worse than an unbalanced budget?" James Curley of Boston, thinking of the bread lines, ugly social disorders, and misery in his city, raised his hand. "Well, Mr. President," he said, "how about a revolution?" Radicals advocate revolution. Conservatives, in their ignorant rejection of several decades of proven fiscal policy effectiveness, would unwittingly bring it about by their insensitivity to the problems of the unemployed.

Yet fiscal policy is only a partial solution to our economic problems. The decline of American output and productivity over the past decade requires much more than an effective fiscal policy, and it also requires much more than the Conservative supply-sider's taxcutting, budget-balancing, and deregulating efforts to "free up" investment and then let growth "trickle down." As we shall see in later issues, expanded governmental policy making in the areas of unemployment, inflation, and investment is needed, not a retreat from policy. We must face the hard facts that not all employment is responsive to fiscal and monetary policy solutions, that not all inflation may be controlled by monetary authorities, and that not all businesses will make proper investment decisions.

The Radical Argument

The debate between Liberal demand managers and Conservative supply-siders has produced considerable confusion among thoughtful Americans. The arguments have usually been framed in either-or terms. Either you intervene to manage the aggregate economy or you don't. Either an unregulated economy works better than a managed one or it does not. Given the record of the past fifty years of American economic history, there is in fact little evidence to make either side's claims very convincing. Thus it is not surprising that modern macro policy debate produces more heat than light. In both actual policy making and the classroom teaching of economics, the result has been "a little of this and a little of that." From a Radical perspective, however, there is no confusion about the issues: both Liberals and Conservatives, albeit for different reasons, are *wrong*.

WHY NEITHER DEMAND-SIDE NOR SUPPLY-SIDE EFFORTS WORK

The fundamental flaw of both Liberal and Conservative approaches begins from the same error: Neither truly understand what powers a capitalist economy. Although both agree that investment is the driving force, each sees investment as depending on different determinants.

Conservatives understand investment as being determined by the level of savings in the society. As savings grow, interest rates (the cost of borrowing) declines, and investors step forward in greater numbers to obtain funds. In turn, their investment actions propel the economy, providing growth and jobs. Accordingly, Conservative policy focuses on actions that will enhance savings. The Reagan tax cut of 1981 was called a supply-side tax cut (although it differed little from earlier demand-side cuts) because it was aimed at giving very large tax reductions to the very rich, who were expected to save their windfall, and to corporations, who were expected to translate after-tax profits directly into investment.* Similarly, Conservatives oppose government deficits that are financed in capital markets in competition with private seekers of funds. Government borrowing is supposed to "crowd out" private investment by raising interest rates. In monetary policy matters, although low interest rates are attractive to investors, too-low rates are opposed because they might discourage saving and encourage consumer borrowing. Therefore, an expansionary money policy is discounted as having no useful effects on investment. In focusing on savings and the interest rate, along with their views on the excessive power of labor unions to raise wage

---

*Although the 1981 tax cut reduced everyone's tax liabilities by 25 percent over three years, the progressive nature of the tax system meant, of course, that the upper-income group paid or was expected to pay a larger share in income taxes. A fixed-percentage reduction on a larger tax liability necessarily meant that the well-to-do received a very substantial portion of the total tax cut.

rates, it is apparent that Conservatives take a *cost-based* approach to explaining how investment takes place and capitalism supposedly flourishes.

Liberals, meanwhile, see the chief determinant of investment as the actual level of aggregate demand. Abundant savings and low interest rates, they argue, will not induce a firm to invest if, as a result of an economic slump, it has a great deal of unused plants and equipment. As demand rises, utilization rates grow, and new investment becomes attractive as the firm actually seeks to expand output. Faced with an underemployed economy, Liberals are accordingly biased toward tax cuts that raise consumption, toward increases in government spending, and under some circumstances toward very low interest rates (which, in their view, encourage borrowing). Their built-in bias focuses on *demand* conditions. Increase demand to stimulate the economy; decrease it to slow economic activity down.

To be sure, Liberals and Conservatives view the economy in its "natural state" in two different ways. Conservatives assume that left to itself and without government tinkering, an economy runs at full employment and near capacity utilization. Liberals view the natural state as being less than full employment but believe that full employment may be reached by means of adroit policy actions. In many other respects, Conservatives and Liberals are quite alike. Both zero in on business investment as the key that unlocks the economy; they differ, however, on their *cost* versus *demand* explanations of why investment takes place. *The difference is a very crucial one.*

To see this point more clearly and to understand why Liberals and Conservatives are both wrong, we must first see that each is "a little bit right" in understanding how capitalism works. *Profit, not savings or aggregate demand, is the real determinant of investment.* Although few Liberals or Conservatives would disagree with the assertion that profit drives capitalism, they fail to see that profit has both a *cost* side and a *demand* side. Remember: *Profit equals sales minus expenditures.* Thus lower costs increase profits and increased sales raise profits, *ceteris paribus*. The trouble, of course, is with *ceteris paribus*.

The very actions aimed at lowering costs (the supply-side menu of cutting the taxes of only the rich, keeping government spending in check, balancing the budget, and so on) lowers demand and thus business sales. Meanwhile, actions intended to increase demand (increased government spending, tax cuts to stimulate consumption, budget imbalance, and the like) raise costs as resource prices are bid upward in an expanding economy. This was precisely the dilemma of the 1970s, as we saw in the last issue.

Ironically, *either* a demand-based *or* a supply-based stabilization policy scenario is doomed to fail in the long run. The problem lies deep in a production-for-profit system. As we saw in the last issue, the normal search for profits produces overproduction and underconsumption crises and falling profits. Efforts to remedy overproduction and underconsumption lead to rising costs and falling profits. In either case, profits, the driving force of the system, are perpetually threatened.

Over the past half century, stabilization policy has been simply a matter of trying now one and now the other of these bankrupt approaches. Although many economists have now tried to reconcile the Liberal and Conservative extremes and build an eclectic system, that is bound to fail too. Invariably, cost-based and demand-based approaches come into conflict. The result is that they either negate each other or one comes to dominate the other.

THE CLASS BIAS AND IRRATIONALITY OF CONVENTIONAL STABILIZATION POLICY EFFORTS

Regardless of its failure, stabilization policy efforts in our time have had one permanent effect: They have erected government as a central feature of the modern capitalist economy. In turn, the modern capitalist state has become a vehicle for class domination and increasing productive irrationality.

Liberals and Conservatives both hold that government policy is capable of being "neutral"; that is, tax cuts or money policy actions, regardless of the particular kind of action, are viewed as having only economic effects. The social and political biases of any of these policies are never put up front for examination. This misses an important aspect of public policy making, namely, that it is a class instrument, a tool for perpetuating ruling-class domination. The social inequalities of stabilization policy are better appreciated by ordinary Americans than most economists admit, but they might usefully be laid out in detail.

First, there is the upper-income bias in taxation policy. A brief survey of important tax-cutting efforts to stimulate expansion—either the cuts of 1964 or those of 1981, for example—indicates that upper-middle- and upper-income taxpayers received the largest percentage reduction and the bulk of the total cut. These same groups, of course, benefit the most from the legal loopholes of the tax system, such as the ability to deduct interest payments and business expenses from their tax bill. The poor and the lower middle class, without the benefits of tax loopholes (or even much opportunity to cheat), have lost economic ground in the tax-cutting efforts of demand-side Keynesians and supply-side Conservatives. In the case of tax increases, the poor again are hit hardest. The recent increase in Social Security withholding taxes is a good example. Over the past few years, both the taxable base and the rate of the taxes have risen at the lower end of the income scale. (In 1986, the rate was 7.15 percent on earnings up to $42,000.) Such taxes are regressive, since they fall heaviest on lower incomes.

Second, low-income Americans have also lost out on the spending side. While Conservatives and Liberals (for different reasons) point to the magnitude of federal transfers to the poor and indigent, this is a massive deception. The federal government's spending in this area amounts to about the same percentage of the GNP today that it did in the pre-Keynesian 1930s.* At the same time, transfers to large farmers, businesses, and professional workers have grown. Government spending for goods, meanwhile, directly benefits the ruling class and higher-income workers. A good example of the upper-income and monopoly-capital bias of such expenditures is military and space spending. The recipient firms are among the largest in the nation and also the most capital- and skill-intensive. Spending funneled into these firms strengthens monopoly power and has little or no impact on creating jobs for less skilled and lower-paid workers (see Issue 4).

Looked at in this way, government spending, even for stabilization purposes, is not neutral at all. It actually heightens class divi-

---

*This fact may seem startling to Americans, who are constantly bombarded with propaganda about the alleged extravagance of social spending on the poor. In reality, we spend only a little over 2 percent of our GNP on programs directed specifically to low-income groups (about $55 billion in 1979). In 1938, for example, the $1.5 billion spent on various poor relief programs by federal, state, and local governments amounted to a little less than 2 percent of the GNP.

sions in the society. Spending on low-income housing, medical care, and other social goods that would improve the poor's quality of life has always ranked very low among fiscal priorities. This is because the poor, regardless of their numbers, are not yet a powerful constituency and also because spending for certain social goods would actually create competition with the private sector. Subsidized public housing would destroy the lucrative low-income housing market in the private sector, free clinics would bankrupt private hospitals, and so on. Moreover, when the stabilization experts call for a contraction in government spending (to balance the budget or reduce aggregate demand), services and transfers to the poor are the first items sacrificed.

While Liberals in the heyday of Keynesian policy were less inclined to cut so deeply or so obviously, the Conservative budget cutters of the Reagan years brutalized the poor. In the name of "trickle-down" economics, poor children were told that catsup now qualified as a vegetable in the school lunch program, and the unskilled were told that there were plenty of jobs in most newspapers' classified sections. Meanwhile, all social service budgets were chopped.

Third, monetary policy is equally selective and unfair in its class effects. For instance, the 1982 pursuit of high interest rates (a tight money policy) as an anti-inflation tool especially burdens the working class. For consumers, high interest rates mean that greater portions of their income must be paid for such necessities as home mortgages and for the "luxuries" provided by credit buying. Upper-income groups, of course, face the same interest rates, but their burdens are a much smaller proportion of their income and more easily borne without sacrifice of their living standards. Meanwhile, for workers, tight money translates into reduced business output and fewer jobs or lower pay.

Thus stabilization policy perpetuates and accentuates the normal class inequalities of capitalism. Expansionary policy never benefits the poor as much as the rich. And contraction always demands that the least affluent American citizens must tighten their belts the most. The normal exploitative tendencies of traditional capitalism are merely reinforced under both Liberal and Conservative approaches.

Apart from the inherent injustices of stabilization policy, there is also the problem of the irrational production and consumption that it encourages. As American capitalism has steadily enlarged its productive capacity—or, in Paul Baran and Paul Sweezy's analysis, its ability to produce surplus—it has had to develop equivalent devices to absorb the surplus. Leaving government aside for a minute, the private sector has devised a number of important ways to "waste" (absorb) output. Developing socially useless goods (hygienic and cosmetic goods come to mind) and expending considerable resources to distribute, advertise, and sell these goods help create jobs and income, but such activities do not elevate society much. Yet such needless and irrational production and consumption, with the attendant creation of needless and alienated labor, do absorb the surplus.

Government spending has pushed along the absorption of surplus through irrational means. Presently, we are spending well over $300 billion a year on military goods—a beautiful way to absorb the surplus. We build machines that have no social usefulness, do not compete with private enterprise, and hopefully will be quickly outmoded so that we can build more. However, people are put to work, corporations earn profits, and the GNP is increased by the spending.

Rather than reconstructing a stable economy, uncritical and unplanned government spending policy has reinforced the irrational production and consumption patterns of a capitalist system.

With government spending now restrained by the force of supply-side tax and expenditure cutting, it would be erroneous to conclude that government has ceased contributing to productive irrationality. By cutting corporate taxes and reducing other burdens on the private sector, encouragement of irrational production and investment decisions has shifted from the spending side of the government budget to the revenue side. The technique differs, but the outcome is the same: more socially useless goods and a more meaningless life for consumers and workers.

THE EMERGING CONTRADICTION

Overall, the past twenty or thirty years of public policy have heightened internal capitalist contradictions. The unequal distribution of benefits and losses has produced growing conflicts—big business versus little business, capital versus labor, worker versus worker, worker versus nonworker, and always rich against poor. And overarching everything is the mounting evidence that government cannot deliver on any of its promises of full employment, growth, and price stability.

The result is a growing public reaction against Liberal government. The temporary rise of worn-out laissez-faire economics, however, may have one positive effect: The Conservatives will reveal the class-biased nature of capitalism much more quickly. As a result, Americans may finally be willing to go beyond the narrow and oppressive economics of their past. When the Conservative ideology fails, as it must, and the Keynesian alternative remains discredited, we will be forced to consider an economic and social agenda we have evaded thus far. Under these circumstances, we will go beyond merely "stabilizing" the economy to reorganizing it and planning it so that oppression and irrationality no longer exist.

Government Deficits and Policy Choices

Does the Size of the Federal Debt Really Matter?

When national debts have once been accumulated to a certain degree, there is scarce, I believe, a single instance of their having been fairly and completely paid. The liberation of the public revenue, if it has ever been brought about at all, has always been brought about by a bankruptcy; sometimes by an avowed one, but always by a real one, though frequently by a pretended payment.

Adam Smith, The Wealth of Nations, *1776*

A decline in income due to a decline in the level of employment, if it goes far, may even cause consumption to exceed income not only by individuals and institutions using up the financial reserves which they have accumulated in better times, but also by Government, which will be liable, willingly or unwillingly, to run a budgetary deficit.

John Maynard Keynes, The General Theory of Employment, Interest, and Money, *1935*

My sum total of economic knowledge is Econ 101 and 102 when I went to college. I've listened to all the Nobel Prize winners for years but I still don't know how we can get along with $200 billion deficits.

Senator Robert Packwood, 1986

Consider the Gramm-Rudman Bill. . . . It is a brainless and gutless piece of legislation. Nearly every professional economist I know agrees with that.

Robert M. Solow, 1985

THE PROBLEM

When Ronald Reagan, elected to the presidency on a platform that promised to balance the federal budget, took office in 1981, the federal debt stood at about $1 trillion. Less than five years later, it had doubled and was growing at such a staggering rate that it was likely to triple before the end of his second administration. The apparent inconsistency between the rhetoric of Conservative budget balancing and the practice of the Reagan years was not lost upon the Democratic candidate in 1984. Walter Mondale worked long and hard to make the growing federal deficit a major campaign issue. He had little success. Perhaps it was because Liberals and Democrats were not, after all, well known for their own budget-balancing efforts: The Roosevelt years had seen the national debt expand ten times over, the Kennedy and Johnson administrations had reported deficits in all but one year, and Carter had never managed a balanced budget. Or perhaps it was because Walter Mondale offered a particularly unattractive remedy to the deficit problem: raising taxes. No one could remember the citizens of the Republic ever having elected a candidate who promised to raise taxes, and Walter Mondale was no exception. At any rate, as it was posed to the voters in 1984, the deficit issue was a nonissue in the campaign.

The election had scarcely receded into history and Mondale into obscurity, however, when virtually everyone from the reelected president to economists of all political hues to the person in the street came to agree that in fact the federal deficit did matter. Some political observers allowed that the deficit had always been a potential issue in the campaign, since growing numbers of Americans were concerned with the growth of the national debt. The trouble was that, rather than exploiting Reagan's vulnerability, Mondale had "shot himself in the foot" by promising to raise taxes to end the deficits. With Mondale and talk of taxes gone, real concern over the debt increased.

Majority economic thinking had come full circle on the debt question in a little over fifty years. The prevailing view in the early 1930s, which had been held as long as economists had been speaking out on the subject, was that government budgets should be balanced annually. Experience had shown that when governments financed spending by printing new money or by borrowing, general economic misfortunes such as inflation, currency devaluation, and general financial instability tended to follow. Ironically, FDR campaigned hard against Herbert Hoover in 1932, lambasting his "spendthrift" opponent for running deficits in the previous two years of depression.

The growing popularity of John Maynard Keynes' ideas in the 1930s and 1940s, along with the actual experience of watching budget deficits grow precisely as the economic gloom of depression receded, caused a shift in opinion. Few economists by the 1960s seriously advocated an annually balanced federal budget. A number talked about cyclically balanced budgets, in which expenditures and revenues should reach parity over a complete business cycle. The focus on the budget in such an approach was to use deficits to finance needed economic expansion while surpluses naturally accumulated during periods of prosperity. Clearly related to this view was "functional finance," which showed no real concern in any accounting sense for balance or imbalance at all but focused exclusively on using debts or surpluses as policy tools. To the functional finance theorists, there was no fundamental limitation on government's capacity to create and finance deficits, regardless of the size of the debt.

By the 1980s, the sudden explosion of the federal debt forced a change in majority economic thinking again. As Table 3.1 shows, both debt as a share of GNP and interest payments as a percent of GNP moved sharply upward. With debt and interest outlays on the debt growing faster than national output and also seeming to accompany an infla-

Table 3.1 Measures of the Federal Debt

Year	Public Debt (billions of current $)	Real Debt (billions of 1967 $)	Debt (% of GNP)	Interest (% of GNP)
1929	16.3	31.9	16	0.7
1940	50.9	121.2	51	1.1
1946	259.5	443.6	124	2.0
1960	290.9	327.9	57	1.2
1972	425.4	339.5	36	1.2
1976	619.3	363.3	36	1.7
1980	914.3	370.5	35	2.4
1982	1,140.9	394.6	37	2.7
1986 (est.)	1,950.0	590.9	46	4.0

Source: Statistical Abstract of the United States, 1985, and Economic Report of the President, 1986.

tionary period of high unemployment and slow growth, many economists (mostly Conservatives at first but soon joined by many Liberals) began to believe that deficits did have an adverse effect on the general economy.

Beginning in the early 1980s, pressure was building for passage of legal restraints on government's capacity to create debt. In its strongest form, this pressure expressed itself as a proposed constitutional amendment that would require annually balanced federal budgets. Whether or not such an amendment will ever be passed remains at this writing to be seen; however, Congress, responding to the popular pressure for budget balance and alarmed by its own and the president's inability to slow the flood of red ink, passed its own version of budget balancing in late 1985. President Reagan quickly signed the Gramm-Rudman-Hollings Act into law. Under the act, a schedule was laid out for obtaining annual budget balance by 1991, with absolute deficit limits imposed beginning with the fiscal 1987 budget. Should budgets come in at higher than allowed deficits, the act called for arbitrary across the board cutting by the percentage of the excess deficit to all spending categories except social security.

Few economists, Conservative or Liberal, expressed much satisfaction with Gramm-Rudman-Hollings' automatic, across the board cutting of spending to meet deficit targets. Indeed, even the constitutionality of the act was uncertain. Critics maintained Congress had acted in a cowardly fashion. Unable to decide politically *what* should be cut when the voting public seemed to be clamoring for *something* to be cut, Congress set up machinery to cut *everything* in equal proportions (except of course, social security).

The Solomon-like wisdom of this approach to balancing budgets was certainly not economic logic—whatever the ideological paradigm—at its best. Conservatives worried about defense spending cuts and insufficient cuts in social spending. The distinct possibility that tax increases and not spending cuts would ultimately be used to meet deficit targets was another Conservative concern. Meanwhile, Liberals and Radicals saw the imposed cuts in social spending as "balancing the budget on the backs of the poor."

While the final chapter is yet to be written on Gramm-Rudman-Hollings, the ideological differences of opinion on deficits and their impact remain. While there is fair agreement among all ideological shades that deficits do matter and that the heyday of "functional finance" is over, there is wide disagreement on the precise consequences of deficits, on their real significance, and on how they might be eliminated.

SYNOPSIS. Conservatives oppose government budget imbalance on the grounds that it is inherently destabilizing, producing inflation, rising interest rates, and reduced private investment. Furthermore, the discretionary nature of demand-management fiscal policy, which they see as the source of the rising debt, is singled out as particularly unwise. Liberals, while concerned with recent trends in debt growth (which they see as the result of Conservative mismanagement), generally view the debt as a tool of fiscal management. Radicals see the debt issue as a reflection of the economy's general inability to realize surplus value. They point not only to the growth of public debt to support this view but also to the even faster growth of private debt.

Anticipating the Arguments

- What is the logic of the Conservative argument that links budgetary deficits with inflationary pressures?

- Explain the Liberal argument that it isn't the size of the deficit that is important, but the way in which the deficit is acquired.

- Why do Radicals maintain that eliminating the deficit is *impossible*?

The Conservative Argument

If there is a particular gauge of the failure of demand-management policies, it must be the federal debt. The growth of the debt and a general indifference to this growth was, until comparatively recently, an aspect of Liberal doctrine that was scarcely ever criticized. Introductory economics textbooks devoted a few pages to discussion of federal debt but quickly moved on to other topics, leaving the distinct impression that "debt doesn't matter." In fact, the debt does matter. Not only is it the undesirable outcome of wrong policy choices, but annual operating deficits by the federal government and mounting aggregate debt also throttle an economy, encouraging inflation and general economic stagnation.

Although Liberals have little understanding of the real problems posed by growing deficits, they are quick to point out that much of the current federal debt was acquired during a Conservative presidency. The implication is that what Conservatives say on the debt question is really just "hot air." The charge is inaccurate and begs the evidence. Although the federal debt did double during Reagan's first five years in office, this debt explosion was in fact the result of pre-Reagan fiscal excesses and the reluctance of a Liberal Congress to cut federal spending. As much as ever, budget balance remains the central objective of Conservative fiscal thinking.

DEFICITS AS A SOURCE FOR INFLATION

One of the more objectionable features of government's running high and persistent annual deficits is its inherent inflationary effect. When government spends more for goods and transfers than it collects in taxes, it increases the total demand for all goods produced in the economy. If an increase in the supply of goods equal to the increase in government-generated demand was instantaneously forthcoming, there would be no problem: more demand, more goods, prices unchanged. However, this is not how an economy works. Even in an underemployed economy capable of producing a greater output by simply adding productive resources, there is bound to be some *demand-pull* inflation as the existing output is bid upward in price. When the economy is operating near full-employment levels, as it was through most of the 1960s and the early 1970s, and when government is at the same time piling up large annual deficits, the demand-pull pressure on prices is very much greater. Approaching the outer limits of the society's actual productive ability, demand increases cannot by themselves raise production.

Apart from their demand effect, deficits also have an inflationary effect through the money supply. Deficits must, after all, be financed. Two options are open: Bonds may be sold to financial institutions and the general public (which creates its own special problems, as we shall presently see), or the Federal Reserve System may purchase the new securities and in turn increase the Treasury's account, providing the government with funds to pay its mounting bills. When the latter takes place, as it will when the Fed attempts to complement an expansionary fiscal policy with an accommodative (and expansionary) monetary policy, new money is created.

To see the effect of monetizing the debt, we need simply understand the traditional explanation of inflation: "too many dollars chasing too few goods."

The long-term growth of output and employment in any economy depends on the society's utilization of resources. Prices are nothing more than the measure by which money is exchanged for commodities. Accordingly, the general tendency of prices in any society will be determined by changes in the stock of money available for transactions. The stock of money, of course, must increase or decrease as the general level of economic output expands or contracts. A relative decrease in money stock compared to output must produce general price reductions. A money expansion rate above the rate of increase in output will lead to price expansion. Quite simply, more money does not and cannot by itself create more goods. Instead, it will be spent on the available goods at higher prices.

This analysis of the fundamental cause of inflation is amply supported by evidence. Every significant inflationary episode in U.S. history has followed excessive growth in the supply of money. However, neither logic nor the evidence has succeeded in deflecting modern state policy from pursuing an inflationary course. As we indicated in our discussions of stabilization policy and unemployment, public policy has been committed too long to the Keynesian belief that high levels of output can be created and maintained by manipulating aggregate demand. Through the 1960s and 1970s, deficits were the intended outcome of fiscal policy. Their excess demand effects were enlarged as the Fed, pursuing an easy money policy, monetized the deficits.

The economy was seized by an inflationary episode it could not control. The sequence of events producing the stagflation of the mid- and late 1970s should be carefully understood. The Conservative analysis of how underlying economic forces are affected runs as follows: The immediate impact of expansionary monetary and fiscal policy will probably be to induce new business investment and additional consumer spending. Thus an increase in output and employment may occur. However, the expansion is only temporary at best. Tricked by a sudden increase in earnings, businesses and consumers have overspent and overborrowed. While money income has risen, their "real" situation has not improved; indeed, it has probably worsened if they have overspent. Over time, however, people learn. Anticipated discretionary actions by monetary and fiscal authorities merely induce businesses and consumers, who are not stupid after all, to take any action they see fit to protect themselves. Their "rational expectations" negate the impact of the authorities' policies. Over time, expansion of the money supply no longer stimulates economic expansion (even temporarily); it simply fuels demand inflation without any employment benefits. In fact, unemployment gets worse. The situation is a bit like a kitten chasing its tail. Excess demand inflation (aided by other Liberal tinkerings with the market) lowers real income and demand for goods, which in turn lower employment. More economic intervention is therefore required to offset these employment losses. This in turn generates more inflationary pressures, which in turn lead to more unemployment. The more the kitten tries to catch its tail, the faster it must run.

THE IMPACT OF DEFICITS ON INVESTMENT AND BUSINESS

As noted earlier, the monetary authorities do have an option other than monetizing the debt. They can sell new government bonds, financing government's deficit spending out of private savings. While this is certainly less inflationary, it has equally undesirable effects. When government goes into funds markets as a borrower, it competes with private borrowers. With increased competition among all borrowers—government as well as private seekers of investment funds—interest rates (which are the price of borrowing) are pushed upward. For business borrowers, the cost of obtaining funds rises. The result is to "crowd out" some private business investment that would otherwise have taken place at a lower interest rate.

The magnitude of the "crowding out" effect is a matter of some debate. A few economists hold that a dollar of government borrowing squeezes out a dollar of private investment. But even if the effect is much smaller, government borrowing adversely affects the productive base of the economy, which is, after all, the real determinant of output and employment.

DEFICITS AND TRADE BALANCES

By the early 1980s, it was apparent that the high and rising federal deficits had yet another undesirable effect: They were adversely affecting our international trade position. We shall examine this problem in detail in Issue 7, so a brief outline here will be sufficient to make the point.

Through the 1970s, accompanying both the deficits and the deficit-generated inflationary pressures was a steady upward push in interest rates. From the point of view of lenders around the world, the comparatively high American interest rates made investment in all kinds of American securities highly desirable. Indeed, a large portion of the new government bond issues, floated to finance the swelling debt, were purchased abroad. To buy American securities, it was essential to obtain American dollars. The resulting demand for dollars pushed upward the price of American currency *vis-à-vis* other world currencies. With a strong and strengthening dollar (some would call it an overvalued dollar), American goods sold at relatively higher prices in foreign markets while foreign goods sold relatively inexpensively in our own domestic markets. With imports rising and exports falling, the balance of trade turned decidedly against the United States.

While it is not accurate to lay all our trade problems at the deficit door, it is obvious that insofar as deficit spending and deficit financing have an upward effect on interest rates, they have helped create an artificially strong dollar, which has translated directly into a worsening international trade position.

DEFICITS DO MATTER

From the foregoing arguments, it should be obvious that deficits have an extraordinary impact on the contemporary economy. Paradoxically, they bring about the opposite of their intended effects. Rather than leading to a demand-powered expansion of output and employment, as Liberals have long claimed, they lead in the other direction toward inflation, rising interest rates, dwindling investment, and ultimately to lower levels of output and employment. Given the political nature of many of the economic decisions that increase government spending and deficits, it is difficult to create a balanced budget through the normal legislative budgetary process. Far too many powerful voting interests have personal stakes in keeping spending high and thus keeping deficits high. Too many candidates for high political office have learned that the briefly stimulative effects of a "political fiscal policy" that pumps up demand just before election time can assure victory at the polls.

The only solution is to establish a firm set of rules with regard to government finance. The passage of a constitutional amendment requiring annual budget balance, except in times of war and extreme national emergency, would end the abuses of discretionary fiscal policy and expedient political decision making that combine to create chronic deficits and bring on economic instability.

The Liberal Argument

Despite the fact that the Reagan years, when Conservative policy influence was at its greatest, saw the doubling of the federal debt, Conservatives still hold to the view that deficits are a profoundly evil economic undertaking. Nevertheless, they are right in stressing that "deficits do matter." What they do not seem to understand, however, is that they matter in *how* and *why* they come into being in the first place. Some deficits matter much more than others.

PUTTING THE SIZE OF THE DEBT IN PERSPECTIVE

The recent focus on the deficit problem has been stimulated by public concern for both the size and the growth of the public debt. However, it is important to understand what the numbers really say. As Table 3.1 indicates, the real growth of the debt before its recent explosion during the Reagan years was substantially less than its nominal (or current-dollar) growth. In constant dollars, the debt was abut the same in 1981 as it had been at the end of World War II. As a percent of GNP, total debt was vastly smaller in 1981 than in 1946. Thus the argument that the growth of the debt was altering the

American economic landscape is not very convincing, since the so-called spendthrift 1960s and 1970s turn out not to have had any impact on the real (as opposed to the nominal or dollar) level of federal debt.

The other misplaced emphasis of the Conservative argument, with regard to pre-Reagan debt accumulations, is to view the debt as a cause rather than the result of general economic conditions. The simple fact is that a troubled economy has produced deficits, not vice versa.

UNDERSTANDING WHERE THE DEBT COMES FROM

Conservative analyses of deficits make little effort to distinguish among different sources or causes of a given deficit. In fact, two major but quite different causes for the federal government's running a deficit are identifiable. First, there are deficits that are directly the result of a general economic slump. When recession strikes, government revenues decrease as taxable income lowers, but expenditures rise automatically as larger numbers of the public begin drawing unemployment benefits and varieties of other transfer payments (including subsidies to business) grow. Even if additional expenditures were not made, a gap between revenues and expenditures would develop since government outlays were planned before the slump and were based on anticipated revenues. This is called a *cyclical budget deficit*. It is estimated that every time the unemployment rate rises by one percentage point in a recession, the loss of revenues and the automatic rise in outlays create a $40 to $50 billion revenue-expenditure gap.

A second, and quite different, source of debt growth may come from a *structural budget deficit*. Structural deficits arise from some discretionary redirection of fiscal policy—the passage of a tax cut (decreasing revenue collections) or the introduction of a huge public works or military spending program (increasing outlays), for instance. Structural deficits may develop as the result of either wise or unwise policy making. They may also result from external conditions over which policy makers have no (or very little) control, as in the case of World War II and Vietnam spending.

With a little reflection, it should be obvious that it is important to know whether a given deficit is the result of cyclical or structural events. Clearly, an attempt to balance a budget in a period of cyclical downturn—either by raising taxes or by reducing government outlays to the needy—is both economic and political foolishness that could make downturns worse *and* destabilize political institutions. In failing to distinguish between types of deficits and in persistently calling for a constitutional amendment requiring a balanced budget, Conservatives are proposing the most destructive possible approach to government budgeting.

While Conservatives oppose all deficits, it is obvious that most of their attack is directed against structural deficits since any manipulation of government revenues and outlays for the purpose of demand management is, in their view, wrong. Their conclusions with regard to such deficits and their effects is easily stated: Deficits, purely and simply, cause inflation and discourage investment. That judgment, however, is not unequivocally supported by theory or empirical evidence.

First of all, consider an economy that has slumped into recession. A structural deficit acquired when an economy is undergoing a cyclical downturn or when substantial underemployment of available resources exists need not create demand-powered inflation. The expansion of total demand resulting from a consciously developed structural deficit under these conditions can put the unemployed back to work and reemploy unused productive capacity without excessively bidding up wage and resource prices. This was the case in the early and mid-1960s. The moderate deficits of the Kennedy and Johnson years (before Vietnam War spending generated demand-inflation pressures) lowered unemployment and stimulated the economy without pumping up prices. Moreover, as we noted in the last issue, most of the inflationary pressure that built up in the late 1970s came not from the demand side and government deficits but from supply-side shocks and cost-push inflationary effects. The Conservative view that all inflation results from excess demand and that government deficits are the primary source for excess demand is simply not supported if the events of the 1970s are honestly reported and evaluated.

Second, structural deficits do not necessarily and under all conditions discourage or "crowd out" private investment demand that might otherwise be forthcoming. If crowding out exists at all, it can take place only when an economy is near full employment and is utilizing virtually all of a fixed stock of investable funds. At any point below this level, "crowding in" is a much greater likelihood, with private investment rising as expansionary fiscal policy puts unemployed resources back to work. As output rises, new investment opportunities develop; they do not disappear.

Third, Conservative logic is empirically contradicted by recent events when Conservatives were having their own way with budget making. Following Conservative reasoning, the enormous deficits following their "supply-side" tax cuts in 1981 which were not matched by spending reductions should have generated enormous inflationary pressures. With the largest structural deficits in American history, we might also have expected the greatest price inflation. In fact, prices did not rise very much. As any good Keynesian would have predicted, the economy expanded, and the cyclical deficit actually shrank.

Given an understanding of the foregoing points, Liberals are not about to cave in to Conservative and popular pressures and dispatch deficit spending to the junkyard of ill-conceived economic policies. Quite to the contrary of Conservative allegations, Liberals have always believed that deficits matter. They matter precisely because, when well planned and executed, they provide an important tool of economic management. However, Liberals also believe that deficits matter when they are piled up as the result of badly executed policies. The defense of deficit spending under certain conditions can in no way be extended to defend the deficits of the Reagan years.

THE REAGAN DEBT FAILURE AND THE BALANCED BUDGET ARGUMENT EXAMINED

The so-called Reagan deficits need to be examined for a number of reasons. First of all, what was their impact on the economy? And second, how did these deficits differ from the deficit spending that Liberals are willing to defend?

Regarding the first question, it is obvious that the loose fiscal policy of the Reagan years did not reflect a very rational approach to macroeconomic management. The doubling of the federal debt in five years did power the economy out of the 1981–1983 recession, but unevenly and with lingering and troublesome side effects. This was true because Reagan fiscal policies lacked a clear focus and were uncoordinated with monetary policy. As the federal budget was hemorrhaging from supply-side tax cuts, the administration encouraged a tight monetary policy to keep down the expected inflationary pressures. The effect was a bit like driving a car by depressing the accelerator and the brake at the same time. The car might move with some degree of control, but the equipment was being worn out. Suddenly it became apparent that as recession lifted and prices held steady, a new problem had arisen. The higher interest rates had created a very strong dollar (that is, the high return on U.S. dollars put the dollar in great demand relative to other world currencies). As other currency values fell relative to the dollar, dollars bought more foreign goods, and domestically produced goods, denominated in dollars, cost more when sold overseas and paid for in cheaper foreign currencies. (We shall examine this problem in more detail in Issue 7.)

Conservatives maintain that the high-interest policy was the direct result of deficits and deficit-inspired inflation. That is true only insofar as a high-interest-rate policy was the ill-chosen Conservative reaction to the nonexistent problem of deficit-inspired inflation. Conservatives had themselves to blame for a strong dollar and the resulting damage it caused to the economy. Ironically, under Conservative mismanagement, the nation succeeded in acquiring two very large deficits—the exploding federal debt and an international trade deficit. Paradoxically, the latter deficit served to negate many of the potentially positive effects of the former. The stimulative gains of an expansionary fiscal policy (even if it was a fiscal policy Conservatives didn't want or understand) were offset by demand leakages resulting from a flood of foreign goods into American markets.

Whether or not the Conservative deficits were well planned or not is, of course, not the really important question. Nor is it really the first question we should ask. The question that reveals the truly important differences between Liberal and Conservative approaches to deficits is, *Why would Conservatives, who advocate budget balance, ever become associated with the greatest debt explosion in American history?*

To unravel the question we need only remember the sources of the expanding deficit, the sequence of events that produced it, and the ultimate objectives of Conservative macroeconomic policy. The source of the Reagan deficit is no mystery. It resulted from two developments that were a critical part of the Conservative program and, when put in place, were bound to create a highly irrational fiscal strategy. As noted earlier, structural deficits could result from well-conceived programs or from wrongheadedness. In the case of the Reagan program, the wrongheadedness is abundantly clear.

The first part of the Reagan fiscal policy produced the personal and business tax cuts of 1981–1983 and a gaping hemorrhage on the revenue side of the budget. The second part of the strategy was the incredible expansion of federal outlays resulting from a 50 percent or greater annual increase in military spending. Although social spending and entitlement programs (i.e., Social Security) are usually singled out as the cause of growing debts, the charge obscures the fact that these programs, under the heaviest budget-cutting pressures, have shrunk as a share of the federal budget.

But wasn't the deficit-expanding effect of cutting taxes and raising spending understood? The answer is yes. It appears that the deficits were acquired by design. Only by making deficits and the size of the debt obnoxious would it be possible eventually to cap deficit spending with a balanced-budget amendment. The sequence of events leading to a trillion dollars of red ink should be understood. *First*, the tax cuts were obtained. *Second*, in the name of defense, military spending was increased. *Third*, growing deficits were accomplished. By giving people something good first—a tax cut and an improved defense posture, it became obvious that the only way the good things could be kept and not have the bad effects of deficits was to cut deeply into government social programs.

Some will say this is ascribing too much perversity and manipulativeness to Conservative politicians and economists. But it is the only explanation that makes sense if ultimate policy goals are to both shrink the size of government and to neutralize fiscal policy by requiring a balanced-budget. In other words, the Reagan red ink was not accidental nor inherited but purposely created to frighten the nation into accepting a shrunken and neutralized role for government in the economy.

As of this writing, it remains to be seen if the strategy has worked. Opinion polls indicate growing public support for a balanced-budget amendment, and Congress has targeted the early 1990s for requiring annual budget balance. From the Liberal point of view there is much to worry about. As we pointed out in the last issue, neutralization of federal fiscal policy would return us to being tossed about willy-nilly by the business cycle. Instead of being able to lean against the winds of cyclical change, government would be required by constitutional law to push in the same direction. Taxes would rise and government spending would fall precisely when demand increases would be needed to offset a slump. And it is at least theoretically possible that an economic expansion could become an inflationary episode as increased tax collections are used to finance greater-than-needed public expenditures. For most Liberals, a legally required budget balance is a leap back in time to an earlier, Neanderthal era of economic thinking.

The Radical Argument

As we noted in the previous two issues, the current stage of capitalist crisis may be distinguished from previous crises by the central role government has come to play in the economy. The other side of the past half century's efforts to use government both as an agent to make up chronic deficiencies in the demand for goods and to lower business production costs has been the steady increase of government deficits. The current deficit crisis and the problems it imposes serve as a measure of the failure of the belief that the normal stagnation tendencies of capitalism can be corrected by government actions.

REACHING THE OUTER LIMITS OF POLICY MANAGEMENT

Keynesians, as we have seen, perceived that the capitalist system could continue to obtain profits only so long as the demand for goods was sustained at high levels. Doubters simply disappeared as the levels of demand were pumped up first by World War II deficit spending and later by the deficits of the 1960s. Rather than competing with the private sector, as classical and neoclassical theory held, government spending (by all levels of government) reduced the pressures of chronic unemployment and excess capacity. It absorbed output and made the private realization of surplus value possible. As Table 3.2 shows, both the absolute magnitude of this spending and government outlays as a share of GNP have continued to grow. Absorbing a mere 7.4 percent of national output in 1903, the government now accounts for more than one-third of the GNP. As we saw in the previous two issues, the expansion of government spending

Table 3.2   Government in the Economy, 1903–1984

Year	GNP (billions of dollars)	All Government Spending (billions of dollars)	Government Spending as a Percent of GNP
1903	23.0	1.7	7.4
1913	40.0	3.1	7.7
1929	103.4	10.3	9.9
1939	90.8	17.6	19.4
1949	258.0	59.3	22.9
1959	486.5	131.0	26.9
1969	944.0	286.8	30.4
1979	2,417.8	750.8	31.1
1984	3,661.3	1,258.1	34.4

Source: Economic Report of the President, 1985.

did slow the system's deterioration into crisis for a while, and while it seemed to work, no one talked much about government deficits. But by the late 1970s, deficits were seen as a source of trouble.

Of course, the trouble is that government spending in general and deficits in particular increase demand but at the same time raise costs to businesses, squeezing their profits. As we saw in the last two issues, the expansionary fiscal policy of the 1960s triggered upward pressures on the prices of resources and on wages. The present Conservative effort (and the efforts of some Liberals) to focus on these bad effects of activist fiscal policy and its resulting deficits merely reflects a redirection of American policy thinking away from the "demand solution" toward searches for a "cost solution" for sustaining profits. It does not represent a theoretical breakthrough for capitalism.

The recent flurry of interest in Conservative supply-side solutions to the capitalist problem is revealing for two reasons. First of all, the demand-oriented policies of the Keynesian era have finally run their course. Government spending must be financed either out of growing deficits or by rising taxes. The former method is inflationary and is severely testing the limits of the financial structure to carry the burden of debt, especially since the private sector is expanding its borrowing even more swiftly than government. The latter method is pushing the taxpayer to the wall. At any rate, both inflation and rising taxes as ways of financing growing government spending are no longer acceptable policy alternatives. The capitalist system, consequently, has reached the limits of fiscal expansionism as a device for realizing surplus value.

Second, the supply-side approach is a bold and naked effort to pick up the pieces of the demand-side failure. The supply-side efforts to cut social spending and to end heavy taxation of the rich and giant corporations are nothing more than an effort to maintain corporate profits by reducing the well-being of practically everyone but the very wealthy. The supply-sider wants not only to reduce taxes and social spending but to roll back wages, permit monopoly power, and end consumer, job, and environmental protection. All such programs, it is argued, interfere with businesses' ability to invest, expand, and make profits. Of course, the supply-siders are right: business *does* need greater freedom (read: ability to exploit) if it is to survive the growing profit squeeze. But if business survives this way, many people will not.

Yet there remains an irony in the supply-side emphasis on the "cost" effects of maintaining high levels of aggregate demand. Like a junkie hooked on drugs, giving up government deficits is difficult, probably impossible, regardless of the degree of human discomfort we are willing to impose on the general population. The fact is that enormous amounts of government spending are not demand-based at all but are directed toward cost-side effects. Spending has grown in a number of ways that are clearly aimed at lowering business operating costs and expanding profits. Military spending, taking up a third of all federal outlays, is first and foremost a kind of subsidy to many very large American corporations. Meanwhile, building highways, subsidizing education, even taking up most of the costs of maintaining adequate retirement and health programs for the elderly, which firms might have to pay for if Social Security did not, all have the effect of lowering business costs. Thus even Conservatives committed to balanced budgets have little real-world success in lowering government outlays and balancing budgets. To make the irony a bit clearer: Like a junkie, the economy needs fiscal fixes to get high, but also it needs them just to stay even.

THE MISPLACED FOCUS ON FEDERAL DEFICITS

The attention directed by both Liberals and Conservatives to the size and growth of the federal debt, predictable as it may be, obscures an understanding of the real problems of the system, of which the debt, like the growth of government in general, is only a symptom.

First, by looking only at the federal deficit, we are deflected from looking at other types of borrowing. The result is a misleading impression because the federal debt amounts to only a small part of total borrowing in the United States, which includes consumer debt, mortgage debt, corporate debt, and state and local government debt as well. In fact, in 1980, federal debt amounted to less than 12 percent of all borrowing. Since borrowing by consumers, businesses, and other government units has precisely the same result as federal borrowing in powering demand, the focus on the federal share of debt is especially myopic. More to the point, as Table 3.3 illustrates, between 1960 and 1980, the period most frequently cited by Conservatives as that in which federal debt expansion first created and then fueled a destructive inflationary spiral, the federal debt grew more slowly than any other component of the nation's total debt. While Conservatives are essentially correct in arguing that borrowing creates "too many dollars chasing too few goods" and thus, sooner or later, inflationary pressures, they simply focus on one small slice of the debt pie. Even if the federal budget were balanced, it would not halt the debt-driven growth of demand.

Second, the Conservative view that federal deficits must be brought under control (a view also supported by many Liberals—though usually for quite different reasons) focuses only on the "too many dollars" aspect of the problem. These theorists do not understand that doing the reverse of what seems to cause inflation or raise

Table 3.3 Outstanding American Debt, 1960–1980 (in billions)

Year	Consumer Debt	Mortgage Debt	Corporate Debt	State and Local Government Debt	Federal Debt
1960	65	207	939	70	284
1965	103	333	1349	100	313
1970	143	474	2084	144	371
1975	223	802	3444	220	533
1980	385	1446	5471	336	907
change, 1960–1980					
	590%	698%	583%	480%	319%

Source: Statistical Abstract of the United States, 1982–1983.

interest rates will not necessarily result in relatively falling prices and interest rates. The fact is that tightening up on debts (federal as well as other) *will* reduce the number of dollars chasing goods. However, as we saw in the late 1970s and early 1980s (Issue 1), it will not necessarily reduce price pressures. Demand may bid up prices initially but prices tend to stay up as a result of businesses continuing old and inefficient (high cost per unit of production) operations. Reducing demand by lowering federal deficits will not signal to business an improvement in general economic conditions. It will not induce them to modernize their production operations and lower their costs by taking on additional investments. As the early 1980s were to show, businesses will have little desire to acquire new investment when they face declining demand (resulting from reducing the number of those "too many dollars"). There would be little point in adding investment that might not be used precisely because demand was being restricted. Only by bringing the economy virtually to its knees, through a deep recession that created enormous excess capacity, was the strong upward pressure on prices halted in the early 1980s. When "few" dollars are chasing whatever goods are available, it is elemental that prices must and do come down.

Finally, government, with its persistent expansion of debt, must be seen for what it really is—simply one aspect of the fundamental contradiction that faces a capitalist, production-for-profit system. The recurring crisis of production outstripping consumption has not ceased in our time. This tendency has simply taken new forms, with the contradiction manifesting itself in the battle over government budgets and fiscal and monetary policy. Indeed, the modern capitalist state is a proxy for capitalism itself. The state budget is the battleground among contending groups in the capitalist economy.

Yet it is a battleground on which victory is unobtainable. We have learned over the past five decades that when overproduction appears (or demand lags), as it chronically does, we may offset it by increasing demand (through government and private borrowing). We have also learned that increasing demand raises costs to firms by stimulating wage and resource price increases. The only cure to the resulting cost squeeze is a full-blown economic slump that will force wages and costs down, one that is very likely deeper and more protracted than would have occurred if demand had not been stimulated in the first place.

Radicals are not confused about what deficits are or what they can and cannot do. First of all, deficits are not the problem. Second, neither deficits nor budget balancing offers any long-run solution to the chronic problems of a production-for-profit economic system.

ISSUE 4

Chronic Unemployment
Is "Full Employment" Possible Anymore?

Once I built a railroad, made it run
Made it race against time
Once I built a railroad, now its done
Brother can you spare a dime?

Popular song by Jay Gorney, 1932

Capitalism forms an industrial reserve army that belongs to capital quite as absolute as if the latter had bred it at its own cost. Independently of the limits of the actual increase of population, it . . . creates a mass of human material always ready for exploitation.

Karl Marx, 1867

There are not enough private sector slots even if employers were given 100 percent subsidies to hire the disadvantaged.

Arnold Packer, Assistant Secretary of Labor, 1979

THE PROBLEM

By the mid-1980s, there was a noticeable indifference among many Americans, at least among those who were working, to discussions about unemployment. Time was, not many years before, that unemployment was viewed as virtually the sole proxy measurement of the economy's performance. Government release of current unemployment data could not only spark a good argument in a neighborhood bar, it could also serve as a quickly assembled lecture topic for economics professors. Rising unemployment was taken as a sure sign that the economy was softening and, in the years of high Keynesianism, a signal that expansionary fiscal or monetary efforts were required. A good deal of macroeconomic thinking—both by economists and by the general public—centered around "unemployment watching."

For economists, the targeted goal was a "full-employment" economy. Needless to say, maintaining high levels of employment (and low levels of unemployment) still remains a central goal in economic thinking, Keynesian or otherwise. The debate over stagnation, stabilization policy, and government deficits explored in the previous three issues, certainly support such a generalization. However, events of the past decade have detracted from the central position of unemployment measurements as the critical economic barometer. First of all, there were the stagflationary late 1970s and early 1980s, when inflation rates and lagging production growth and investment accompanied high unemployment. In many economists' and ordinary citizens' minds, inflation and falling productivity were every bit as significant as unemployment as immediate measures of economic well-being. Second, unemployment itself began to respond somewhat differently than it had in the past. Full employment had never meant 100 percent employment. Economists of all political persuasions understood that not everyone would be at work, even in a prosperous economy. Below some minimum unemployment level, any effort to force unemployment lower would translate into demand-inflation pressures without many employment gains. In a sense, a little unemployment was needed to lubricate the economy. In the 1950s, experience showed that "full employment" was about equal to a 3 percent unemployment rate. By the 1960s, full employment was redefined at about 4 percent unemployment. In the 1970s, it was revised upward to 5 percent and, in the 1980s, to 6 or 7 percent (a few Conservatives thought it might be as much as 8 percent). The constant upward revision of full employment somewhat reduced the usefulness of unemployment as a measure of cyclical economic activity. Periodic unemployment fluctuations always had to be adjusted to consider the high and rising proportion of unemployment that was considered "chronic."

We have directed our attention thus far to policy efforts to deal with cyclical economic shifts and their attendant impact on employment. We now turn to the problem of growing "chronic unemployment," worklessness that seems to have little or no connection to the economy's general level of performance. We may have become a bit hardened to this issue, but it remains an important dilemma of modern public policy.

The stubborn rise of unemployment rates requires directing attention to identifying the unemployed and determining why they cannot find jobs in the economy. Looking more closely at unemployment, we can see it is unevenly distributed. It is greater among blacks than whites, among women than men, among teenagers than people 25 to 40, and among the unskilled than the skilled. It is higher in the older industrial states of the East and the Midwest than it is in the South and Southwest.

Moreover, as Figure 4.1 indicates, the problems of the chronically unemployed have not diminished much when the economy has periodically picked up. Unemployment for minorities, teenagers, and women has remained consistently high, even during the comparatively good years of 1973–1974 and 1976–1978.

If this persistent joblessness is not responsive to economic growth, what are the means to solving the chronic unemployment riddle? Whatever the solution, all of us must realize that a society that cannot or does not find work for its people is in deep trouble. The ideological battle over how to attack the problem of chronic unemployment is more than just an intellectual debate.

SYNOPSIS. Conservatives see the present unemployment problem as largely the result of government efforts to manage labor markets. They therefore advocate minimum government involvement as the only long-run solution to joblessness. Liberal arguments hold that much of our current unemployment is beyond the reach of usual stabilization policy tools. Thus new and enlarged job programs are necessary to remove the "structural" limitations of the economy that have created chronic unemployment. For Radicals, unemployment is characteristic of capitalism, a natural outgrowth of the system's tendency to produce surplus labor.

FIGURE 4.1 PROFILE OF THE NATION'S UNEMPLOYED, 1972–1984

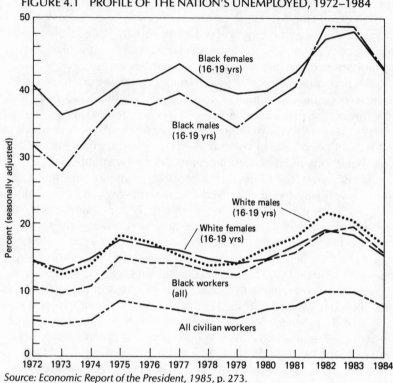

Source: *Economic Report of the President, 1985*, p. 273.

Anticipating the Arguments

- How, according to Conservatives, have government actions *increased* unemployment?

- What do Liberals mean by "structural unemployment," and how would they cure it?

- Why do Radicals believe that high levels of unemployment are characteristic of a capitalist system?

The Conservative Argument

From the Conservative point of view, unemployment is logically unnecessary. In an economy left to its own devices, involuntary unemployment can result only from short-run market readjustments. The classical economist Jean-Baptiste Say (1767–1832) argued long ago that supply creates its own demand. Say presumed that demand naturally would remain high and that work would be available for everyone who was willing and able. Say's world, of course, no longer exists. As has been pointed out before, massive interruptions in the market have become institutionalized. In the world of labor unions, big government, and discretionary fiscal policy, Say's Law has little relevance. The Conservative critique therefore must begin with the macroeconomy as it is.

A RISING "NATURAL RATE OF UNEMPLOYMENT"

At all times, a "natural rate of unemployment" exists. At the natural rate, employment is just enough so that no wage and price inflation results from a short supply of potential workers and the economy is in equilibrium. In the idealized world of Jean-Baptiste Say, the natural rate was understood to be about zero since all wages and prices were assumed to be freely flexible and workers free to go wherever they liked in search of work. As a result, some job always existed at some wage somewhere for anyone willing to work at that wage. Individuals who thought their services to be worth more than was bid for their labor and accordingly refused employment were "voluntarily unemployed" and therefore not reflective of the economy's capacity or incapacity to create jobs.

In our era, the natural rate of unemployment has been rising, perhaps to as much as 7 or 8 percent of the labor force currently. The source of the problem is not really surprising, and it certainly *is not* proof that "capitalism doesn't work." Rather it reflects how our economic system has been adversely affected by a variety of efforts originally intended to improve on the market economy's performance. The natural rate of unemployment is high and rising because prices and wages *are not* flexible and because labor *is not* very mobile.

The lack of wage flexibility and labor mobility are the results of past Liberal efforts to intervene in the economy. However, presently concerned about rising "chronic" unemployment, they propose elaborate solutions that will guarantee greater unemployment and greater resource misallocation. To see the point, we need only examine a few of their past efforts.

THE RECORD OF A FAILED EMPLOYMENT POLICY

To see how labor markets have been made less mobile and less flexible and therefore characterized by a rising natural rate of unemployment, we shall look at four areas of Liberal tinkering: support of unions, social legislation, antidiscrimination efforts, and efforts to offset structural change.

Liberal support for labor unions in this century, while benefiting some workers, has cost many their jobs. Unions, by instinct and design, restrict the number of jobs as they force wages upward for their members. The older craft unions specifically used the tactic of exclusion in forcing higher wages. By having long periods of apprenticeship and limiting the number of apprentices, unions in the building trades, for instance, purposely reduced the supply of available labor. This kept carpenters', masons', and hod carriers' wages up, but it also kept large numbers of would-be workers out of the labor force. Meanwhile, large industrial unions also reduce employment. By forcing upon management an industry wage that is higher than would otherwise prevail in a free labor market, the industry's total demand for labor is reduced; thus both wages and unemployed workers increase.

Legally mandated social legislation (unemployment insurance, workers' compensation, Social Security contributions, etc.) also depresses employment. Ironically, many of those programs aimed specifically at the poorest and least secure workers have worsened rather than improved their lot. For instance, Liberals invariably cite the passage of minimum-wage laws as one of their greatest triumphs; yet such laws have probably had the largest negative impact on employment of all of their efforts at social engineering. Setting minimum-wage rates above a market-determined wage has two immediate effects. First, more individuals enter the labor market, now willing to work at the higher wage, whereas they opted for leisure before. Second, the number of jobs available is reduced, since employers cut back their hiring. While minimum-wage legislation has been defended by Liberals as a boon to the less skilled workers, it has actually had the opposite effect. The least skilled jobs, those with the lowest marginal contribution to a firm's earnings, must be the first eliminated as the result of raising the minimum-wage floor. Thus part-time employment for teenagers and unskilled factory work for women and minorities have declined as the minimum wage advanced.

The Liberal charge that discrimination is a major cause of unemployment has brought forth a number of elaborate affirmative action programs, all of which produce expensive paperwork for corporations but have not reduced minority unemployment. (In mid-1985, black unemployment was reported at about 20 percent, more than twice that of whites and higher than it was two decades earlier.) The trouble with the Liberal analysis is that it misinterprets minority unemployment. While Conservatives admit the existence of past discrimination in education and in the general society, they reject the argument that employers consciously discriminate. For that to be the case, employers, who are, after all, profit maximizers, would have to pay additional costs for the act of discrimination. Excluding certain elements of the workforce as undesirable (minorities or women, for instance) would reduce the supply of available labor and force up the price of labor in general. This would not benefit employers. However, it would benefit white male workers in general and unions in particular.

Recent efforts to apply a doctrine of "comparable pay for comparable work"—whereby jobs traditionally filled by women and paying low wages would be priced upward toward wage levels of allegedly "similar" jobs traditionally filled by men—constitute the most recent Liberal and Radical delusion about how to cure "discrimination." Never mind that there is no other mechanism than the market itself to determine "worth"; reformers plan to impose wages on the basis of their own views of equity. The result, if such a program is actually developed, will be to increase unemployment since many workers' wages will simply be greater than the value of their contribution to the firm. Ironically, women are likely to be the real losers.

Periodic and quite natural shifts in the economy's structure produce short-run unemployment from time to time. Buggy makers do not become auto workers overnight, and auto workers cannot immediately be transformed into computer specialists. However, it is possible to make a temporarily bad employment situation permanently worse. Recently, declining employment in the old, moribund basic industries—steel, automobiles, and farm machinery, for instance—has encouraged Liberals to call for special aid programs for the hard-hit industrial centers of the Northeast and Midwest and for direct aid to the old and failing industries. Such aid may in fact lower unemployment for a time, just as aid to buggy makers would have softened the unemployment effects of Henry Ford's Model T production. But it also has the socially undesirable effect of halting economic change. By subsidizing old and inefficient industries, we must tax the vital sectors in the economy. Detroit and Gary are kept afloat, but jobs are reduced in the high-tech centers of Texas, California, and Massachusetts.

The Liberal proposal for special job programs to deal with varieties of structural unemployment is both unnecessary and counterproductive. Despite two decades of federal expenditures for the education of young people, the retraining of older workers, and elaborate public service programs, as well as affirmative action programs to increase the employment of minorities and women, there is virtually no evidence that significant numbers of would-be workers have been aided. In fact, the tax bill for funding and operating these programs has probably had a negative impact on jobs, because private-sector funds had to be shifted to these employment efforts.

The best cure for so-called structural unemployment would be to free up labor markets, to reduce union power, to eliminate the minimum wage, and to let the chips of technological change fall where they will. If there is structural unemployment, it is caused by imposed higher wages and inefficient government employment programs, not by the fact that there is a real shortage of potential jobs for workers.

UNEMPLOYMENT IS OVERSTATED

Unemployment is certainly higher than it should be and than it would be without current government policies; however, the level of joblessness is overstated rather than understated. The advantages of welfare and unemployment compensation have attracted many who would not otherwise enter the labor market. More than that, certain types of job seekers—particularly those who are merely supplementing the family income—should not be counted in the same way as the primary jobholder in a family. While they should indeed have work if they want it—and could in a society freed from fiscal interference and such labor market constraints as unions, minimum-wage laws, and social "protections"—unemployment as presently reported overstates the importance of their problem. It suggests incorrectly that work for all is impossible under capitalism. Under pure capitalism there would be jobs; under the present mixed economy there is unemployment.

The overreaction to unemployment statistics has also tended to direct attention away from positive employment developments. Even with the high unemployment statistics of recent years, the number of *employed* workers has been growing steadily. Between 1980 and 1985, all supposedly high-unemployment years, the total number of employed workers grew by 8 percent, from 99 million to 107 million.

Thus if we understand who is unemployed and why and if we also recognize the real vitality of the economy in employing workers, the current high levels of unemployment can be put in a more balanced perspective. Nevertheless, Conservatives do not defend high natural rates of unemployment. A lost day's work is a loss to the society forever. However, the natural rate of unemployment and lost days of work will remain high so long as interventions in labor markets and the economy in general prohibit labor markets from developing flexibility and workers from exercising mobility.

The Liberal Argument

Of the almost 12 million Americans out of work in late 1982, a large share owed their joblessness to the recession engineered by the Reagan administration. Their unemployment was the "cost" of Reaganomics, the ruthless application of monetary brakes and budget cutting aimed at drying up inflation. About 5 milllion of these unemployed would find work by 1985. While their forced idleness was painful and largely unnecessary, it was not hopeless. For the others, however, even the return of good times would make little difference. Their unemployment was not the result of insufficient demand; rather it was the result of subtle institutional changes in the American economy. The problems of unemployment require a new approach. Not only do we need policies to cure lack-of-demand joblessness, but we must recognize that some unemployment is chronic and not responsive to demand increases.

STRUCTURAL UNEMPLOYMENT

Since World War II, the American economy has enjoyed, with a few brief interruptions, phenomenal economic growth; however, the expansion has produced important technological changes and regional economic shifts that have contributed to national unemployment. The demand for older jobs and skills has declined as new goods and production techniques have revolutionized labor. At the same time, the geographic distribution of manufacturing has been altered. Meanwhile, the old employment bulwarks—steel, autos, and construction, for example—are undergoing a deep structural decline, both as employers and as contributors to the nation's output, which few observers believe will soon reverse. The result has been to change the structure of labor markets.

Here are some examples of these structural shifts:

1. The continued decline in agricultural employment as farm production was increasingly mechanized
2. The increased use of more and more sophisticated technology in industrial production, thus reducing the relative demand for industrial labor in general and unskilled labor in particular
3. The migration of many businesses and factories from the inner cities to suburban locations
4. The greater concentration of economic activity in large metropolitan areas and the decline of employment in smaller cities
5. The shift in the geographic location of industry to the West and South as new industries grew up in these areas and old plants left the industrial Northeast
6. The sectoral shift in employment patterns as service industries and government increased employment and the old

employers—in manufacturing, transportation, mining, and construction—declined. (In 1950, manufacturing, transportation, mining, and construction employed more than half the workforce; by 1980, these industries employed less than a third. Meanwhile, over the same period, service and government employment grew from 25 percent to over 40 percent of all employment.)

Across the nation, the structural changes in employment produced large pockets of chronic unemployment. Since most of those unemployed lacked sufficient skills, or at least the skills needed, economic expansion of the economy had little effect on their work status. Pumping up aggregate demand would not have much effect on an unemployed railroad worker in Altoona, Pennsylvania, an out-of-work miner in Kentucky, or an ex-steelworker in Gary, Indiana.

THE CHANGE IN LABOR FORCE COMPOSITION

Changes in the composition of the labor force have added to the structural problems. Beginning in the 1960s, larger numbers of women began to look for work. Most of these new entrants possessed minimal skills and took, when they could get them, low-paying jobs in the service sector with little employment security. Many of the female job seekers were extremely immobile. Many were wives and mothers who had to seek work near their homes. This added a further restriction to their general lack of skills in obtaining work. Meanwhile, the entrance into the job market of the large number of people born in the post–World War II baby boom increased unemployment. As with women, many of the youthful job seekers did not meet the new employment demands. For urban, primarily black, youths, there were virtually no jobs at all. They had no desired skills and, anyway, they did not live near or have access to the few unskilled jobs available.

REJECTING THE RADICAL AND CONSERVATIVE CRITIQUES

The addition of these new entrants precisely at the time of great structural changes in employment markets inflated unemployment rates. The incorrect impression was created and championed by Radicals that the growing unemployment reflected the chronic incapacity of the system to create jobs. However, if we understand the real causes of chronic unemployment, the problem lay with the workers and not the economy in general. Quite simply, too many would-be workers lacked the education or were in the wrong location to find work.

The Conservative argument that unions and minimum-wage laws have restricted employment is utterly false. For most of the chronically unemployed, there would not be jobs no matter how low the wage level. Industry no longer hires just bodies but demands a highly educated labor force. There are serious shortages in the labor market for tool and die workers, machinists, accountants, bookkeepers, engineers, computer programmers and operators, and other skilled workers. Lower wages, as Conservatives argue, will not open these jobs to the chronically unemployed. Wages are not the issue; skill levels are. Proof of this may be seen in the fact that the minimum wage, as a percent of average factory earnings, is smaller today than it was during either the long boom of the 1960s or during "Eisenhower normalcy." Evidence does not support the Conservative claim that the minimum-wage law is the cause of our chronic unemployment.

A LIBERAL PROGRAM

As we have noted, structural unemployment and joblessness resulting from changes in the composition of the workforce are not responsive to efforts to pump up aggregate demand. Instead, specific job-creating programs are necessary to provide full employment. However, unlike the make-work efforts of the past (such as WPA in the 1930s), these programs should not be mere bandaids. Since lack of skills is the primary cause of chronic unemployment, federal programs should be constructed to improve the hirability of would-be workers.

A number of job programs offer real opportunities for the so-called unemployables to join the labor force: youth programs, public service jobs, and wage subsidies.

Youth Programs With unemployment among teenagers the highest of all groups (16 percent among white teenage males and 40 percent among black teenage males), youth unemployment demands special attention. Teenagers account for about one-fourth of all the unemployed. Most teenage unemployment, especially among blacks, is found in urban areas. Also, among the teenage unemployed there is a high educational dropout rate. Thus employment programs for this group should be urban in focus and organized to encourage completion of public education. While learning useful skills, many youths will learn the workplace discipline that is necessary for retaining employment. At any rate, a long-run improvement of youthful unemployment problems is fairly certain as the past decade's declining birth rate makes itself felt in labor markets. With a modest jobs program now, youthful unemployment can be brought under control.

Public Service Jobs   Beginning in 1973, the Comprehensive Employment and Training Act (CETA) instituted federal funding for local government hiring of public workers for limited employment periods. Rather than creating an overloaded federal bureaucracy, this approach allowed local communities to set and meet their own public service needs. Workers, meanwhile, obtained important on-the-job experience before their CETA jobs expired. The dropping of these programs during the years of Reaganomics has been a harsh blow to workers lacking skills.

Wage Subsidies   A third approach to chronic unemployment is to subsidize private-sector employment of the unskilled. The bonus paid to private corporations is intended to offset the expected lower productivity of workers in this program.

Be aware that the emphasis on retraining and upgrading skills in both public- and private-sector programs will not immediately affect structural unemployment; nevertheless, over time the effects on improving workers' job opportunities and their productivity should be evident in reduced chronic unemployment. However, real changes will be seen only if the commitment to these programs is much greater than at present. Largely a victim of budget-tightening pressures, the employment program that started with great promise has been scaled down to a fraction of what was originally proposed. This amounts to reversing our national commitment to full employment. Unless our full-employment goals are reaffirmed, chronic unemployment will grow, and the nation will be denied the contribution that these would-be workers could make.

THE COST OF UNEMPLOYMENT

Failure to deal with the unemployment problem will be a considerable cost for America—in both human and economic terms. In human terms, chronic unemployment erodes morale and self-esteem. Studies indicate that periods of prolonged unemployment destroy incentives and interest in work, even when the worker is later reemployed. Without employment, personal behavior patterns become erratic, leading to increased marital and family problems and greater child abuse. Unemployment also increases morbidity, mental illness, and crime. According to one study, a 1 percent increase in the unemployment rate will be associated with 37,000 deaths (including 20,000 heart attacks), 920 suicides, 650 homicides, 4,000 state mental hospital admissions, 3,300 state prison admissions.* While it may be difficult (but not impossible) to put precise price tags on these human costs, we can measure the external or social costs of unemployment that result from (1) reduced tax collection, (2) rising unemployment insurance outlays, and (3) greater plant closings. When all these costs of permitting chronic unemployment are considered, the costs of special job programs to eliminate or reduce unemployment become insignificant.

The Radical Argument

Both Conservatives and Liberals misunderstand the role of unemployment in a capitalist society. To the Conservative advocating a free market economy, there would be virtually no unemployment if the market were to work freely, that is, unimpeded by government action, labor unions, and so on. To the Liberal, unemployment is at least a periodic, and perhaps a chronic, condition of capitalist economies, but it can be controlled by "enlightened" public policy. Neither position sees unemployment as central to capitalist organization, as necessary to the actual functioning of the system. The simple fact is that capitalism, regulated or unregulated, cannot help but create unemployment.

*Barry Bluestone, Bennett Harrison, and Lawrence Baker, *Corporate Flight: The Causes and Consequences of Economic Dislocation* (Washington D.C.: Progressive Alliance, 1981), p. 20.

UNEMPLOYMENT: CAPITALISM AS USUAL

As capitalists accumulate and successfully translate past labor into what they see as profit-producing capital and investment, the need for an absolute or growing volume of labor diminishes. This must be true by simple definition. The object of capital development is to increase production without increased (or with decreased) costs. Labor-saving machinery is cost-saving machinery only because labor is paid less per unit of output. More output can be obtained by employing more capital and less labor. Thus increased capitalization and technological growth, all things being equal, must produce growing surplus labor. This is the historical tendency of capitalism.

The growth of unemployment tends to be in recessionary clusters rather than in a steady, unbroken upward movement; however, the overall unemployment trend is upward over a period of time. Since the mid-1950s we have seen the official unemployment rates (which are themselves statistical understatements of the problem) move relentlessly higher even in comparatively "good" years. In other words, the percentage of the labor force in what Marx called "the reserve army of the unemployed" is constantly expanding. No doubt this unemployment would have been even higher in the past two or three decades had not government pursued expansionary policies. In other words, the situation has been getting progressively worse despite elaborate governmental efforts to hold unemployment down. Neither the free market nor Keynesian tinkering halts this tendency.

The failure of expansionary fiscal policy to deal with the problem of chronic unemployment is particularly evident if we go back to the tax cut of 1964. This was perhaps the first self-consciously Keynesian effort to use fiscal policy to reduce unemployment (then at 5 or 6 percent). The $11 billion Kennedy-Johnson tax reduction did spur business investment and increase national output. Between 1964 and 1966, investment increased by over 22 percent—more than twice the rate of the previous two years. The gross national product grew by 13 percent during the same period, compared to a growth rate of less than 10 percent in the earlier period. However, reported unemployment fell by only 900,000 between 1964 and 1966, despite the fact that government alone increased its payroll by 1.7 million persons. Thus any real reduction in unemployment came not from tax cutting à la Keynes but from good old government hiring.

An additional case against the supposed effectiveness of "full-employment" fiscal policy is the hyperexpansion of government spending that took place during the Vietnam War. Although government policy during the war may now be represented by Liberals as unintended and undesired (in other words, determined on political rather than economic grounds), it did not result in the employment growth that modern Keynesians associate with expansionary fiscal policy. Between 1966 and 1969, during the height of war appropriations, unemployment fell by less than 100,000. Meanwhile, direct government employment added an additional 1.6 million to public payrolls. Direct government hiring, not private-sector job growth, brought unemployment rates down during the middle and late 1960s.

The point of these cases should not be misunderstood. Fiscal expansionism does create demands for workers. After the 1964 tax cut, during the Vietnam War boom, and after the 1981 Reagan tax cut, unemployment rates did fall a bit. But in each case, "normal unemployment" (what Conservatives euphemistically call the "natural" rate of unemployment) leveled off at a higher level: 3.5 percent in the mid-1960s, 5 percent in the early 1970s, and 7 percent or more in the mid-1980s. What was happening was that "full employment" was being achieved at successively higher levels of normal unemployment, with the pressures of an expanding economy having no useful effect on many workers who were falling out of the employable labor force altogether.

CAPITALISM BENEFITS FROM UNEMPLOYMENT

Political rhetoric to the contrary, the fact is that capitalism benefits from surplus labor—at least to a certain point. Surplus labor tends to force wages downward or at least to slow upward pressures. Workers compete with one another, and employers have a pleasant buyer's market. Even the prospects of important union wage gains are diminished by the competitive threat of the swelling ranks of unemployed. Recently, corporations have shamelessly used the specter of growing unemployment to force the labor union elite of the working class to sign new contracts with important "give-backs." Wage gains and fringe benefits struggled for in the past were wiped out as rising unemployment weakened the unions' bargaining position. The old-line management bargaining tactic of "take it or leave it" was once again successful.

Meanwhile, the Conservative Reagan Congress allowed the consumer price indexing of minimum-wage rates to lapse. By 1985, the $3.40 minimum wage was equal to a mere $1.50 in 1975 dollars. Since the minimum wage in 1975 had been $2.10, this represented a 20-percent real-wage reduction. The logic for holding down the minimum wage for millions of American workers not protected by unions was the usual Conservative line: Higher minimum wages would only cause greater unemployment.

Aside from using unemployment to hold down workers' wages, joblessness also was used to pump up business subsidies. In typical "trickle-down" reasoning, the enterprise-zone program was launched in 1982. In seventy-five designated inner cities, corporations were granted tax reductions and allowed to hire at less than the legal minimum wage. The justification: Jobs would be created for the "unemployables"; the effect: greater profits for corporations while plain old exploitation grew.

UNDERSTATING THE PROBLEM

Bad as it appears to be, our unemployment problem is really much worse than we realize because we understate the number of unemployed in at least four ways. First, the average annual rate does not show the number of people affected by some type of annual unemployment. For instance, in 1982 at least 40 million Americans experienced some unemployment during the year. Looked at this way, unemployment touched almost 40 percent of the American workforce during the year. Even if the unemployed suffered only a week or two of lost labor, the effect could be devastating on savings, retirement plans, and the educational hopes of the worker's children. Second, our statistics tend to overestimate the actual number employed. In 1985, the "employed" included 16 million Americans who worked only part time and another 1.5 million who fell into an "unpaid family labor" category. Such calculations expand the total "employed" category but do not show how slight their employment is.

Third, official statistics do not indicate the underemployed. At least 8 million full-time workers earn wages below the official poverty income level. Fourth, the "unemployed" category does not include workers who are "not presently looking for a job," although they may be people who want jobs but have given up looking. How many people have given up looking? No accurate figures are available, but it is estimated that if this group were added to our known unemployment, 1985's more than 7.1 percent rate easily would have reached 12 to 14 percent.

It is important to understand not only the real size but also the composition of unemployment in the United States. Clearly, job possibilities are poorer if one is black, female, or young. This discrimination in employment is not surprising. Basically, it reflects the general contraction of labor markets and the resulting exclusion of newcomers. On the one hand, such discrimination has served the system well, since many of the unemployed are not visible but hidden away in ghetto or home. On the other hand, obvious discrimination of this kind creates considerable political development among the affected groups, who quite consciously and correctly see themselves as an exploited class. Liberals, aware of this tendency, have proposed make-work and on-the-job-training programs aimed at quashing the discontent of the hard-core unemployed. But such programs have no long-run effect on improving employment.

There is obviously a limit to how large the surplus labor army can grow—not just an economic limit but a political one. Unemployment breeds contempt for the existing order and sows the seeds of revolution. Therefore, capitalism faces the constant problem of devising expensive "legitimation" schemes. Ironically, given our soak-the-poor tax structure and the present fiscal crisis, employed workers are increasingly burdened by taxes to support unemployed workers. This situation has so far only set workers against nonworkers, rather than uniting all against the system that oppresses them.

In any case, modern public policy can do nothing about the threat of long-term unemployment. Short-run manipulation and trade-offs with inflation (see the previous issue) are possible, but the structural foundations of capitalist unemployment remain. Nor do special job-creating programs for the chronically unemployed offer a long-run solution. At best, they only buy a little time through deceptive but unfulfilled promises of future jobs. Small wonder that officials have no wish to tabulate all the unemployed. But their statistical manipulation does not change the historical tendency of capitalism.

RADICAL STRATEGY: EXPOSE THE SYSTEM

The Radical strategy in the face of chronic and growing unemployment must be to halt the self-conscious division of the labor force into workers and nonworkers. As long as the unemployment problem is minimized, either politically or economically, to disguise capitalism's failure, workers will bite each other and not the master as they fight for the system's scraps. A broad educational and political program is necessary to reveal the inability of capitalism to create jobs and to remove the stigma of uselessness from those who cannot find work. Only then can the mass of citizens see the need to end capitalism as a system. Specifically, this means a coalition of employed and unemployed, one that will reject the idea that there is anything left in the Liberal toolbox to fix things up. Some people will say that this is no solution but mere Radical rhetoric. In the absence of a viable Radical political movement, the accusation is more true than false. But only through such educational struggles can a Radical alternative begin to emerge.

ISSUE 5

The Military Budget
How Much for Defense?

> In the councils of government, we guard against the acquisition of unwarranted influence, whether sought or unsought, by the military-industrial complex. The potential for the disastrous rise of misplaced power exists and will exist.
>
> *Dwight D. Eisenhower, 1961*

> Today it is more likely that the military requirement is the result of joint participation of military and industrial personnel, and it is not unusual for industry's solution to be a key factor. Indeed, there are highly placed military men who sincerely feel that industry is currently setting the pace in the research and development of new weapons systems.
>
> *Peter Schenck, Raytheon Corporation, 1969*

National solid waste = $43.5 billion = B-1 bomber program
treatment program
Total environmental = $105.2 billion = New weapons systems
cleanup   in development or pro-
                                                      curement
To eliminate hunger = $5 billion = C-5A aircraft
in America   program

> *Seymour Melman,*
> *National Cochairman of SANE, 1974*

We have not asked for more than we need. This budget merely allows us to meet our basic requirements.

> *Casper Weinberger,*
> *Secretary of Defense, 1985*

THE PROBLEM

There was a time—long forgotten by most of us—when military spending took a very small proportion of a very tiny federal budget. That was, of course, before World War II and the four decades of cold war anxiety that have left an indelible mark on recent American history. To see the economic impact of national security spending, we need only know that the United States has spent well over $2 trillion on war, threats of war, and anticipated wars over the past forty years. In fact, we have spent more than half that total in the past six years. But how much is too much, and how much is enough spending for national defense? The answer is not an easy one.

As Table 5.1 shows, defense spending spurted upward during the Vietnam War years (1966–1972) and then slowed down as a brief rapprochement was obtained with the Russians and after the United States and China ended their long-standing enmity. In recent years, though, the cold war has been heating up. The failure of SALT (Strategic Arms Limitations Talks), growing Soviet military adventurism, deteriorating political

Table 5.1   National Defense Spending, Selected Years, 1939–1986 (billions of dollars)

Year	Amount	Year	Amount
1939	$ 1.9	1974	$ 77.0
1944	84.4	1975	83.9
1949	13.2	1976	86.8
1955	38.4	1977	94.3
1960	44.5	1978	110.0
1965	49.4	1979	123.9
1966	60.3	1980	142.0
1967	71.5	1981	150.1
1968	76.9	1982	181.3
1969	76.3	1983	221.1
1970	73.5	1984	278.1
1971	70.2	1985	316.0
1972	73.5	1986 (est.)	331.0
1973	73.5		

Source: Economic Report of the President, 1986.

conditions in the Middle East and Central America, and the Reagan administration's promise to be "second to none" in military strength all have caused an enormous increase in defense expenditures.

For the remainder of the 1980s, the debate over how much is needed for defense promises to be a hot one. At one level of argument, there is a question of whether or not the atomic powers already have achieved "overkill"—a situation in which mutual destruction is assured regardless of additional armaments. Strictly speaking, this isn't an economic issue, except insofar as additional military spending would be pure economic waste if overkill really is our military situation. However, in the recessed economic conditions of the early 1980s, defense spending did have some clear economic ramifications, irrespective of being purely "defense" questions. Rising defense outlays put great stress on efforts to curb the growth of federal deficits. There appeared to be a kind of cruel irony in President Reagan's 1982 plan for a three-year, trillion-dollar effort to build up the U.S. military. Such spending seemed certain to undermine his balanced-budget objectives. By the mid-1980s, the federal budget was in fact running up deficits just about equal to the Reagan defense budget increases.

SYNOPSIS. The Conservative argument maintains that defense spending, although probably characterized by some waste, is necessary for national security. The Liberals have tended to be divided on military spending, with some opposing the growth of a powerful military-industrial complex and urging that war spending be shifted to social goods, while others, like the Conservatives, have argued for the necessity of a large arms budget. The Radical argument holds that our economy depends on war for profit and maintaining high levels of demand and that shifting this spending to other areas is politically and economically impossible under the present system.

Anticipating the Arguments

- On what grounds do Conservatives exempt defense spending from arguments they offer against other dimensions of government economic activity?

- What do Liberals mean by their argument that defense spending develops "its own constituency" within the economy? How does this constituency act to protect defense expenditures and even waste?

● Why do Radicals believe that large defense budgets are peculiar to a capitalist society?

The Conservative Argument

By any rational calculus, war is wasteful and uneconomical. Human labor, lives, and resources are used not for production but for destruction. Markets are distorted, shortages develop, and the price mechanism fails to direct resource allocation properly. The production of war goods, meanwhile, subtracts from the society's accumulation of capital and its social and private wealth. All of this should be obvious. Yet predominant in most discussions of military spending, or the so-called military-industrial complex, is the charge that war is necessary or that war is good for the economy. Needless to say, this argument is usually advanced by critics of capitalism. It is demonstrably false, but proving logically that war is not essential to a capitalist economy is not the end of the matter. War and threats of war are a reality today. War spending, therefore, is not a function of limited capitalist economic options. It is a necessary political and societal response to an external threat—in this case, the protection of American capitalism and democracy from the threat of international communism.

Although military spending is basically the political problem of a society protecting itself, such spending clearly has economic effects and so should not be beyond the pale of economic analysis. In this area a great deal of confusion exists.

A NECESSARY EXPENDITURE

A common charge is that defense spending is too high. In absolute magnitude, the defense budget is large. The high technological and capital costs of the nuclear age, however, reflect requirements that have changed a good deal since soldiers threw rocks and spears at one another. It must be remembered too that the limits on military spending are not being determined by how much we want to spend but by how much our adversaries force us to spend for adequate defense. More important, though, is the fact that defense spending, while recently rising to meet real defense needs, is relatively small by past standards.

In 1985, the defense budget ran to $316 billion, or about 34 percent of total federal outlays. This was up from the 24 percent share in 1980, when the nation was being stripped of its military strength, but it was well below the 40 percent share in the Vietnam War year 1970. In fact, between 1970 and 1980, proportional defense spending had been steadily declining, while human resource outlays rose from 37 percent to 52 percent of the budget. As a share of the nation's total output, 1985 defense spending was a scant 8 percent. Compare this with, say, 1922. The United States was then at peace, pursuing a foreign policy of isolation, blissfully allowing its army and navy to grow obsolete, and beginning a long period of economic prosperity. Nevertheless, the $1.2 billion spent on defense that year still amounted to 2 percent of our GNP and 35 percent of federal expenditures. The facts simply don't support the alarmist claims of those who oppose defense spending. (One might ask, parenthetically, why these opponents attack military spending—which has been small and until recently has been growing relatively smaller—while showing little concern about government spending in other areas.) Another point about the "size" of military spending needs to be made: Inflation, not real increases in defense buying, is the cause of most military budget growth. As Figure 5.1 indicates, real dollar outlays have scarcely risen since 1976.

FIGURE 5.1   REAL AND CURRENT DOLLAR DEFENSE OUTLAYS, 1976–1987

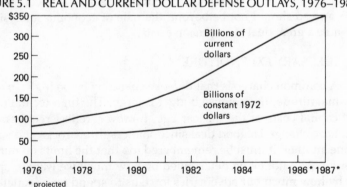

projected

Source: Office of Management and Budget.

Table 5.2   Constant (1978) Dollar Outlays for Defense by the United States and the USSR, 1971–1980 (in billions)

Year	USA	USSR	USSR Advantage
1971	118	120	+12
1972	117	134	+17
1973	112	140	+28
1974	112	147	+35
1975	109	151	+42
1976	103	158	+55
1977	108	159	+51
1978	108	161	+53
1979	112	166	+54
1980	129	169	+40

Source: Statistical Abstract of the United States, 1984.

Since defense is primarily a function of how one's adversary reacts, it is important to ask what the Soviet Union is doing. According to estimates of the Department of Defense and private researchers, the Russians are devoting about 10 to 12 percent of their GNP to military outlays. Such an effort is about twice as great as ours in terms of the share of GNP. As Table 5.2 shows, the Soviet Union consistently outspent the United States during the 1970s, acquiring a dangerous advantage in ICBMs, missile warheads, missile submarines, tanks, and virtually all other indicators of military strength. This, and this alone, has been the determinant of our own recent decision to increase defense spending.

IN DEFENSE OF DEFENSE

A second charge leveled at military spending is that it is inefficient. This is somewhat harder to refute, since there is evidence of cost overruns and technological failures. The problem is calculating efficiency in making military hardware. The production and sale of sophisticated war goods cannot take place in a competitive market; things have changed since Lincoln's secretary of war took bids on horse blankets and salt pork. No rational executive will risk capital by speculating in the tank or missile business.

Secrecy, complex technology, and capital demands set constraints on the supply side of the military market, while the demand side is limited to a single domestic buyer and a few overseas purchasers. Given the reality of monopoly in the supply and purchase of military goods, the record of waste does not seem extraordinary. (One might ask again why critics single out the inefficiency of military spending but neglect to apply the same standards to government purchases from other industries. Is there no waste in highway construction or in federally funded and managed urban renewal and housing projects? Of course war is a waste, but the charge of economic inefficiency is another matter.)

This same obsession with the military and the so-called military-industrial complex appears in charges of conflict of interest and political manipulation. Opponents of military spending talk darkly about the "senator from Boeing," disproportionately high outlays in the districts of certain members of congress, and the ease with which retiring Pentagon colonels slide behind corporate desks. Yet they rarely identify other congressional figures as the "senator from Corn" or the "congressman for the AFL-CIO." No one expects Interstate Commerce Commissioners to be former Boy Scout executives. It should surprise no one that military officers drift toward defense industry jobs.

This is not to defend inefficiency or conflict of interest. Neither should be allowed. But the military is no more guilty than other sectors that deal with government. Such problems are not unique to the "military-industrial complex."

A final word might be said on behalf of indirect benefits from the military budget. Despite the ultimate waste of war and some probable inefficiency in procurement and production, defense spending has produced useful inventions and innovations. Military research and development has made possible, among many other things, Boeing 707s and 747s, our satellite communications network, and the transistor.

Lest readers mistakenly conclude that the Conservatives' position on military spending is inconsistent with their attitude toward government, it should be pointed out that war and defense are decisions that transcend the marketplace. A permanent war economy certainly extends government into areas of social activity better left to the people. This issue calls for vigilance, but defense of the society is essential. This stubborn fact is totally ignored by the opponents of defense spending.

THE MILITARY-SOCIAL SPENDING TRADE-OFF

The Liberal charge that a tank or a missile system has an unseen opportunity cost in the form of lost hospital beds, unfed children, and deteriorating highways is pure propaganda and not good economics. From the Conservative perspective, military spending and social spending are easily separated within a budget, and each deserves its own consideration. The bloated social budget requires reduction for many reasons that we have stated in other issues (see the next issue). These reductions in social spending are important in their own right, not as trade-offs with military hardware. However, the Liberal approach to the question has indeed been to see the matter as a trade-off. When it became obvious that the "guns and butter" policies of the 1960s and early 1970s were not possible without causing an explosion of federal debt and inflation, the guns were sacrificed. Liberals, not Conservatives, initiated the trade-off approach to military and social spending, and the defense of the American people was the casualty.

The Liberal Argument

Conservatives correctly argue that adequate military defense is not a matter of purely economic choice or of frivolous luxury. Quite simply, it is necessary in the cold war (and sometimes hot war) environment in which we have lived for nearly four decades. However, the abstract need for defense and the present dimensions of the military-industrial complex (MIC) are two different questions. As retiring President Eisenhower prophesied in 1961, big military budgets have created a dangerous symbiotic relationship between the Pentagon and broad areas of the American economy. Because of the political influence of the MIC, serious examinations of its extent and inner workings have been difficult. Despite these difficulties, we *must* ask such questions as How much defense is needed? How well is defense spending managed? and How much should defense claim as a share of our national output?

WASTE BUYING AND PAYING TOO MUCH

Although Liberals are not in agreement on how much defense is necessary in dollar terms, some have made a convincing argument that our preparedness for total war has already reached the overkill stage—that absolute numbers of missiles, bombers, and other weapons are no longer a significant measure of our well-being. There is no such thing as a comparative advantage in weapons after a certain point in defense development. When the overkill stage is reached, additional amounts bring no additional security.

Another dimension of overkill is its impact in distorting the development and utilization of labor, resources, and productive facilities within the domestic economy. The well-heeled defense contractors easily hire away the best and the brightest American engineers, scientists, and skilled workers for work in war-oriented industry, depleting the stock of human capital available for nondefense fields. Research and development funds, meanwhile, are readily available for war goods research at precisely the same time they are in short supply in many basic American industries.

Apart from the problem associated with buying too much, there is also the problem of paying too much for what we get. The public purse is ever open to ill-planned and unneeded weapons. During the "low-budget" defense years between 1953 and 1965, more than $10 billion was spent on weapons that proved useless. In the exploding defense budget of 1983, monies were included for the M-1 tank (cost: $2.5 million each), the F-18 bomber (cost: $32 million each) and the B-1 bomber (cost: unknown, but some experts estimate that the first fleet of one hundred would go at nearly $1 billion each). These outlays were proposed despite the fact that all three of these systems had important critics within the military who doubted the actual future effectiveness of the weapon. Included also in the 1983 budget was continued development funding for the Sergeant York antiaircraft cannon, an item finally dumped by the Defense Department in 1985 as "totally unbattleworthy"—after $1.8 billion had been spent on the project.

Even if most of the weapons procured eventually prove out on the battlefield, there is the incredible problem of cost effectiveness in their development and procurement. Awarded handsome cost-plus contracts, prime contractors have a long record of continually piling up cost overruns that have tripled or quadrupled original estimates for weapons systems. The M-1 tank was originally programmed to be built at one-tenth its current delivery price. Defense contractors have little or no reason to maintain cost efficiency in weapons production. Indeed, being efficient would reduce the contractors' gross revenues and, with fixed profit formulas, reduce their total profits. In some instances, as illustrated by the discovery in 1985 that General Dynamics was fraudulently billing the Defense Department for work not actually done, defense contractors have gone beyond mere inefficiency and involved themselves in theft of public monies.

Despite the undeniable record of waste and mismanagement that characterizes military goods procurement, Pentagon budgets have long remained sacrosanct. No part of the federal budget enjoys such intensive congressional and industrial lobbying. The public is fed a steady diet of information and misinformation about new and wonderful weapons systems, missile gaps, and the intentions of our adversaries. Behind the patriotic appeals is the simple matter of dollars and cents. A great many giant American corporations are dependent for their existence on military orders. Lockheed, General Dynamics, McDonnell-Douglas, Rockwell International, Raytheon, and Ling-Temco-Vought—all among the nation's top hundred manufacturers—have depended on national defense spending for more than half their total sales for over twenty years. To a lesser degree, dozens of other firms feed at the Pentagon trough.

Naturally, the military economy affects many citizens. Some 7 percent of all employed Americans work in defense industries; over 20 percent of all manufacturing personnel are involved directly in military hardware. In states such as Connecticut, California, and Washington, about 40 percent of the manufacturing workers are in defense-related industries. The extent of various states' dependence on the defense dollar is illustrated in Table 5.3.

The military-industrial complex is not limited to prime suppliers and their employers. In areas of the country where defense spending is large, people see themselves as having a stake in the defense budget. In a single city or community, loss of a defense plant is understood to have unemployment ripple effects throughout the local economy. When the Air Force recently announced a plan to close its early-warning system in Duluth, Minnesota, the owner of a local fro-

Table 5.3 Where the Defense Budget Gets Spent

	1984 Total (billions of dollars)	Per Capita (dollars)
District of Columbia	1.9	3,123
Hawaii	2.4	2,280
Virginia	12.0	2,137
Alaska	1.0	1,968
Connecticut	6.0	1,895
California	40.0	1,559
Missouri	7.6	1,523
Maryland	6.4	1,462
Massachusetts	7.9	1,356
Kansas	3.2	1,294
Washington	5.2	1,201
New Hampshire	1.1	1,146
Mississippi	3.0	1,142
Utah	1.7	1,010
Georgia	5.8	989
Arizona	1.8	950
New Mexico	1.3	932
Texas	14.3	897
Colorado	2.6	824
South Carolina	2.6	784
Florida	8.2	751
Rhode Island	0.7	739
Maine	0.8	732
Alabama	2.8	703
North Dakota	0.5	693
Delaware	0.4	677
Oklahoma	2.1	636
Louisiana	2.8	632
New Jersey	4.7	627
New York	10.8	609
Indiana	3.3	594
Nevada	0.5	584
North Carolina	3.5	569
Arkansas	1.2	528
Minnesota	2.1	501
Pennsylvania	5.4	457
Kentucky	1.6	431
Vermont	0.2	423
Nebraska	0.7	413

Table 5.3 (cont'd)

	1984 Total (billions of dollars)	Per Capita (dollars)
Ohio	4.4	409
Wyoming	0.2	396
Michigan	2.5	359
South Dakota	0.2	331
Tennessee	1.6	329
Montana	0.2	299
Wisconsin	1.3	265
Idaho	0.3	263
Illinois	3.0	261
Oregon	0.5	204
Iowa	0.6	194
West Virginia	0.2	112
United States	197.4	836

Source: Statistical Abstract of the United States, 1985.

zen pizza company led an entourage of outraged citizens to Washington. When Rockwell International was lobbying for its B-1, they contacted some 5,000 subcontractors in forty states, asking them to write to members of Congress on behalf of the big bomber.

As a result of the great dependence of so many firms and individuals on military spending, it is politically difficult, perhaps impossible, for the waste in defense spending to be examined honestly and openly. Quite apart from the morality of war and the real needs of defense, the military budget also means jobs and profits. Unless we can step back and look objectively beyond our personal interests in jobs and income, defense budgets will remain beyond critical economic examination.

DEFENSE SPENDING AND THE ECONOMY

Radicals have long charged that war is the only way a capitalist economy can cure its periodic problems of recession and depression. According to this view, government spending for war helps maintain high levels of aggregate demand. Moreover, as military spending and war goods investment continue over time, there is a steady shift in production possibilities toward a permanent war goods foundation. The economy is supposedly geared to a certain war production that must be maintained for industry's sake.

Such a view is highly mechanical. It fails to realize that government spending could also be allocated for social goods. Moreover, war goods always diminish a society. In a fully employed society, war goods can be produced only by giving up civilian goods. In our present stagflation economy, persistently large military budgets lead to a serious trade-off with other social spending. When overall federal spending is held down by fears of inflation and limited revenues, big military budgets mean less for education, health, welfare, and other social spending.

With such costs forced upon the society by military spending, it would seem that a shift of government spending from war to social goods is not only possible but essential if MIC power is to be controlled. While such a move may cause some grief and readjustment at General Dynamics, it is not the end of the capitalist economy.

Spending on bombs, tanks, and missiles could just as well be spending on hospitals, parks, or the environment. And unlike war spending, which does not create beneficial or consumable goods, spending in social areas not only benefits the public but also stimulates consumption spending for private goods. This in turn encourages private investment, which is not stimulated (except in defense industries) in a war economy.

Spending on social goods could more than make up for any general economic contraction that might result from reducing the military component of government spending. Economic growth does not depend on war, cold or hot; it would, in fact, be enhanced by a shift toward "peace" goods.

Alas, though it is easy to show the emptiness of the Radical argument that war is necessary for capitalism, it has not been easy to reduce the military budget. Even as his administration was about to be overwhelmed by a flood of red ink, Conservative Reagan would not consider reducing military spending to balance the budget. Instead, the budget was to be balanced by lowering social spending. The contradictions of the Conservative position should not be overlooked. Federal deficits, so opposed by Conservatives, just about equaled the increases Conservatives gained in defense spending during the early and mid-1980s.

In the debate over whether national priorities should favor defense spending or social spending, Liberals feel that social goods must be given preference—short of reducing American defense to ineffectiveness. Specifically, this means taking a hard line against the overzealous MIC lobby. The government must be rigorous in setting standards for procurement policies and enforcing contract terms. Such measures should deter bribery and collusion and stimulate cost efficiency in the firms that do defense business. Steps should be taken to curb the special influence of members of Congress representing regions that depend on defense spending. The deleterious effects on business of reducing or holding the line on military spending could be offset if the government directed other government spending into affected locales and instituted job-retraining programs.

Basically, this program is political, not economic. It is primarily a matter of convincing people to spend money for social goods rather than for war. Its success ultimately depends on the popular will.

The Radical Argument

America's high levels of military spending are not simply the consequence of maintaining an "adequate" defensive position, as Conservatives argue. Nor, as Liberals would have it, are they the largely accidental result of efforts by a self-aggrandizing and small political clique known as the military-industrial complex. On the contrary, military spending and/or war is essential to American capitalist development.

AN OFFENSIVE DEFENSE

In the first place, military spending is not purely defensive—at least not in the sense of building a retaliatory force to negate the "Russian threat." Although the possibility of a Russian attack has been emphasized for four decades to justify military budgets, defense preparations have always entailed much more than a threatened confrontation between the United States and the Soviet Union. When American policy makers have spoken of defense, it has usually been in terms of "defense of the free world." The "free world," of course, is that part of the globe where American capital has interests to protect. Freedom—other than the freedom of American business to manufacture and sell profitably and to obtain resources cheaply—has very little to do with this defensive strategy. Friendly repressive regimes in Chile, South Korea, and elsewhere must be defended from national revolutions that would seize or nationalize U.S. corporate assets.

When necessary, as in Korea and Vietnam, the United States has shown a willingness to invest its young men and its military might to protect its international economic interests. This aspect of military policy is neatly avoided by Conservatives and Liberals. Forgetful they may be, but it is not difficult to recall that both world wars in this century—and most smaller wars in the past two centuries—were either between expansive and competing capitalist powers or between capitalist powers and developing economies that were challenging their hegemony. The basis for war has been capitalist imperialism.

Armies and navies are crucial for capitalist countries in defending their overseas interests. The costs of maintaining these forces and of fighting actual wars are extraordinary. In fact, in any rational sense, the total expenses are usually far in excess of any benefits gained through overseas profits. In the case of Vietnam, one study has indicated that the war may have cost as much as $1 trillion.* While the actual budget for direct war spending was only about $171 billion, to this amount should be added $305 billion for future budget drains for equipment replacement, $71 billion for calculable human losses to Americans, and about $380 billion for the costs of war-generated inflation, recession, and foreign trade problems. Such spending in a war we didn't even win indicates that capitalist "defensive" policies are not rational. Nonetheless, in terms of the system's views of its overseas needs, military waste is essential, even when the waste is a crushing blow to the nation's economy and people.

WAR: A CRUTCH FOR THE DOMESTIC ECONOMY

Leaving aside the supposed overseas benefits from "defense," it is also important in stabilizing the domestic economy. In a micro-

*Robert Warren Stevens, *Vain Hopes, Grim Realities* (New York: New Viewpoints, 1976), pp. 163–196.

economic sense, many firms and some entire industries are wholly dependent on the Pentagon budget for their profit margins. This is not simply a matter of firms that do 50 percent or more of their business with government. Large companies such as General Motors, General Electric, Ford, and Chrysler—which gain less than 20 percent of their sales from military contracts—depend on these contracts for the lion's share of the profits they earn in the United States.

In a macroeconomic sense, high levels of defense spending have been a crutch for the whole economy—a fact acknowledged by the Liberals. They argue that government spending could be used for social rather than war goods. Theoretically, this argument is true, but it fails to consider the political nature of the military budget and the powerful role of corporations in determining governmental fiscal priorities.

The Liberal argument, in underestimating the importance of war spending, neglects history. As even Liberals will admit, it was not the elegant theories of Lord Keynes that led our economy out of the Depression. It was massive wartime spending, not the purchase of social goods, that pumped up aggregate demand and created full employment. While social spending might have had the same effect—at least in theory—the point to remember is that war spending was the route the nation followed. Nor has it altered that course. Conservatives, meanwhile, who disavow any desire to use any type of spending for the purposes of ''stimulating demand'' and who maintain the importance of a balanced budget in fiscal matters, have been the prime movers in the recent expansion of military spending—even though the MIC spending increases have largely been the cause for failure to obtain a balanced budget.

Military spending, from the corporate point of view, is especially attractive *because* it is wasteful. In other words, it produces income and profits while doing nothing to improve or change the society's stock of consumable goods. There is no need to worry about gluts of commodities that will sooner or later be blown up or abandoned. Social spending, on the other hand, is particularly disruptive. In producing certain goods (public power or public housing, for instance), it competes directly with the private sector. Too extensive social outlays also interfere with labor markets, driving labor costs upward.

The profitability of wasteful government spending on military hardware is, from business's point of view, an undeniable factor in its constant lobbying for more "defense" and its cold war "educational" efforts. The public treasury is opened to corporate plunder and profit in the name of patriotism and national security. Business will not easily give all this up.

Up to this point the arms makers have enjoyed much support from labor and certain defense-oriented regions of the nation as they work to maintain military spending and trade it off against social outlays. While the AFL-CIO leadership still remains strongly defense-oriented, there are signs that American workers in general are reexamining the blind commitments to defense spending. Chinese-American rapprochement and the bitter aftertaste of the Vietnam struggle have weakened the "better dead than Red" mentality that gripped the United States for so long. While American reaction to the Russian incursion into Afghanistan showed that cold war hysteria has not ceased entirely, it is important to remember that Afghanistan did not escalate into a Korea or a Vietnam. Popular support for a direct confrontation with the Soviets was less than universal, despite the frequent efforts of American politicians to stir up American jingoism.

At home, the growing power of the MIC aggravates the problems of ordinary citizens in an already troubled economy. Military spending, going primarily as it does to large firms, strengthens monopoly power. Since most war suppliers also produce civilian goods, monopoly pricing power is enhanced in the market for civilian goods as well. Meanwhile, since war production is capital-intensive and complex in its technology, each defense dollar spent produces very few employment gains. Among the hard-core unemployed, military outlays produce no job gains at all. Even for skilled workers, military purchasing and the arms industry are having a declining impact. Thus the long-enjoyed "jobs effect" of the MIC is on the wane.

If Americans can gain a more reasoned understanding of the phony ideological arguments upon which the MIC has been built and perpetuates itself, they can appreciate its real economic effects. Contrary to Liberal rhetoric, however, there are few possibilities of simply shifting public outlays to other areas; at least, there are few possibilities without restructuring the entire economy and society. War is waste, but capitalism depends on waste. The capitalist system is inherently unable to opt for rational and humane production. The ability to wage war protects capitalism's interests overseas, and the system cannot exist without these interests. Realization of these facts, along with an understanding of capitalism's chronic tendency toward unemployment and inflation, reveals the profound irrationality of the American social and economic order.

ISSUE 6

The Social Budget
Can Social Security Survive the Crisis in Public Finance?

Among our objectives I place the security of men, women and children of the nation first. . . . Hence I am looking for a sound means which I can recommend to provide security against several of the great disturbing factors in life—especially those which relate to unemployment and old age.

Franklin D. Roosevelt, June 8, 1934

All in all, Social Security is an excellent example of Director's Law in operation, namely, ''Public expenditures are made for the primary benefit of the middle class, and financed with taxes which are borne in considerable part by the poor and the rich.''

Milton Friedman, 1980

Cutting back on benefits will undermine people's faith in the integrity of the whole system—they will feel double-crossed.

Wilbur J. Cohen,
former HEW official, 1981

I can't live without Social Security and I can't live with it.

Shirley Deitchman, retiree, 1982

THE PROBLEM

The second largest expenditure item in the federal budget, after national defense, is Social Security, amounting to about $200 billion in 1986. Created in 1935 at the depths of the Great Depression, the Social Security System epitomized the New Deal era's commitment to maintaining individuals' social welfare. As the years have passed, the Social Security System—its benefits, coverage, and place within a growing federal welfare structure—has undergone great changes, but it has not lost its premier position within the federal social budget. However, the American Social Security System is in trouble.

The problem has two parts. First, there is the more immediate problem of rising Social Security outlays in a time of serious fiscal crisis. Since 1978, Social Security cash payments have more than doubled. A variety of reasons can be offered to account for this sudden surge of payments: inflation (which has meant that benefits, indexed as they are to cost of living changes, had to rise), the enlargement of certain individual benefits in the late 1970s, and the increased number of recipients in a quickly aging and longer-living American population. After a brief political debate in the early 1980s over whether or not the nation could afford its existing Social Security System, we appear to have at least postponed the immediate funding problems through a combination of increasing participant contributions, shifting trust funds from certain Social Security programs to those most quickly exhausting their previously accumulated resources, and through some minor reductions in Social Security benefits. However, in a time of enormous federal deficits, it is possible that a funding crisis could break out again.

The second part of the problem is longer-term, but at some point down the road, the immediate problem and the long-term problem merge. The combination of increased life expectancy, the eventual retirement of the "baby boomers" of the 1950s and 1960s in the first couple of decades of the twenty-first century, and the relatively low recent birth rate will eventually produce a ratio of beneficiaries to contributors that must cause funding difficulties. In fact, the rise in this ratio is well under way. In the 1950s, there were seventeen employed persons for each Social Security recipient. By the 1970s, there were only about three. Estimates (assuming no important changes in the law) project that by the

FIGURE 6.1 PROJECTED BENEFICIARIES PER HUNDRED COVERED WORKERS, 1980–2050

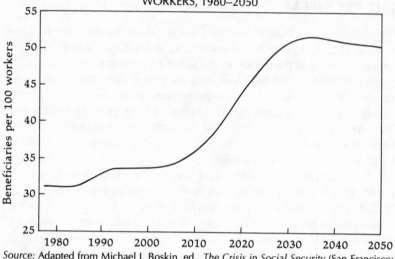

Source: Adapted from Michael J. Boskin, ed., *The Crisis in Social Security* (San Francisco: Institute for Contemporary Studies, 1971), p. 8.

third decade of the twenty-first century, there will be about two workers for each retiree (see Figure 6.1).

The problem posed by these trends is obvious: Just how shall we pay for our Social Security System? Initially, the program was to be operated like a giant insurance policy. Contributions by workers and employers were to be paid into several trust funds (Old Age Benefits, Medicare, and Disability), with each worker receiving benefits according to what he or she had paid in. For years, the trust funds bulged deceptively, with more paid in each year than was paid out in benefits.

As time passed, however, a number of the original Social Security premises have been changed or abandoned. First, the original self-funding approach was replaced gradually by paying current retirees out of current tax collections. By 1975, we had reached the point where one year's Old Age outlays exceeded that trust fund's total resources. Second, benefits were disconnected from the amounts actually paid into Social Security by individuals. Third, the benefits were expanded very greatly—far beyond an actuarial projection of payroll tax payments by individuals and employers. What does all this mean? Quite simply, it means that current tax revenues, including current Social Security taxes, essentially pay current benefits. Or, to be very blunt, two unknown young readers of this book can look forward to the day when they shall be supporting the author out of their current Social Security tax payments.

Can we continue to operate the Social Security System as we have known it? Does our generosity need to be tempered by a new economic reality? Must we abandon altogether our fifty-year-old commitment to sustaining the elderly and the infirm? The brewing fight over this biggest slice of our social budget pie promises to break out at any time, not only setting ideology against ideology but even age group against age group.

SYNOPSIS. Conservatives maintain that the defenders of the Social Security System have fraudulently promised elderly Americans a retirement income that simply cannot be afforded by the nation. Meanwhile, the very concept of an "involuntary" Social Security program erodes individuals' rights and operates as a drag on the entire economy in its discouraging of private savings. Liberals respond that Social Security is both a solemn promise and the only protection that many have from abject poverty in their declining years. Liberals also maintain that the fear of the Social Security System's going bankrupt is a pure scare tactic used by its opponents. Radicals see the eventual sacrificing of the Social Security System as an illustration of the fiscal crisis confronting government—an inability to provide both outlays that benefit capital *and* expenditures for people's needs. Thus Social Security and other social outlays must be reduced constantly.

Anticipating the Arguments

- On the basis of what evidence do Conservatives maintain we cannot "afford" the Social Security program?

- How do Conservatives and Liberals disagree on the question of an individual's responsibility and choice in the matter of providing for retirement?

- Why do Radicals believe that the growing attack on the Social Security System really masks a fundamental problem in state financing? What do they see as the cause of this problem?

The Conservative Argument

The Social Security System was the first and remains the biggest program in the American version of the welfare state. It is therefore appropriate to focus upon the Social Security System in any general discussion of the social budget and the fiscal and economic crisis posed for the nation by enlarged social spending. As with most social programs, Social Security is an excellent example of how we have been deluded and manipulated since the incipient drift toward welfare statism began under Franklin Roosevelt. Ironically, most Americans simply do not understand that Social Security and other "giveaway" programs are pushing the national economy to the brink of disaster. It is not simply a "type" of program that Conservatives oppose for philosophical reasons. The opposition is based on simple economic sense. As we have said before, there is no such thing as a free lunch. And the cost of the Social Security banquet, despite its immense popularity, is prohibitive.

MYTH VERSUS REALITY

The managers and political supporters of the Social Security System have created a number of self-serving myths about their program that persist in spite of common sense and overwhelming evidence to the contrary. Perhaps the most enduring myth is that Social Security is merely an insurance program, in which government holds tax payments in a pool and then pays them out on an actuarialized basis, just as a private insurance company would. Even a catchy and inventive TV commercial on behalf of the Social Security System perpetuates this belief when it announces: "It's your money!" Nothing could be further from the truth. We long ago abandoned the insurance-fund approach to the Social Security System. What remains of the old funds (Old Age Benefits, Medicare, and Disability) will be exhausted in a few years. The fact is that Social Security is operated on a pay-as-you-go basis; consequently, nothing is accumulated. No investment of funds is made, and there is no accumulation of interest—things that, after all, make it possible for private insurance companies to operate not only solvently but profitably.

A pay-as-you-go system means it isn't "your money" if you retire, but someone else's. Your money, meanwhile, is—or will be—going to support someone else. On the surface that may seem fair enough, as long as someone else's money is there when you have retirement needs. Okay, maybe it isn't an insurance system, but it's pretty close, right? Wrong! With retirement benefits (skipping the various nonretirement programs of Social Security) being paid out of current taxes *and* exceeding the actual contribution of the retiree (since benefits tend to grow much faster than contributions), it is obvious that retirees are receiving more than they themselves paid in. In other words, they are getting transfer payments from those who are productively at work. The simple fact is that a Social Security pensioner is just as certainly on "welfare" as is an AFDC mother or a food stamp recipient.

All this leads to a second myth: that the retirement monies, whether provided by an insurance or a welfare system, will be there for you when it's your turn to receive. It seems fair that if you pay for someone else, someone should pay for you. However, for this to be possible, the contribution rate has to expand constantly (unless benefits are cut, which, of course, wouldn't be "fair"). Given the demographic profile of the population, the number of recipients is growing far faster than the number of contributors. The situation is a bit like the old pyramid game or a chain letter: If you are near the bottom of the list, your money contribution or required number of letters tends to expand geometrically over that required of those above you. As long as the pyramid or chain isn't broken behind you, you will do all right. But like the pyramid or chain letter, the burden for those on the bottom sooner or later becomes too great compared to the estimated rewards, and the link is broken. It is a simple political fact that the relative level of benefits for Social Security retirees will not be continued when contributors are faced with an excessive burden and little hope that they will ever get back anything like their contributions. There is no economic "proof" that workers in the year 2000 won't pay the 30 to 50 percent of their salary needed to sustain retirees at present standards, but it seems likely that such demands on workers will be politically unacceptable.

Meanwhile, the immense popularity of the Social Security System, as well as the economic difficulties it is in, largely stem from another myth: that the Social Security System was intended, by itself, to provide all of us with a comfortable standard of living when we cease working. Even by Franklin Roosevelt's liberal standards, Social Security was supposed only to provide "safeguards from misfortune." Framers of the act did not have in mind sending retirees to Florida condos to bask in the sun. Social Security was only to protect the very poor and elderly from total destitution. It was, for the more fortunate, to be a small bonus to their personal retirement savings. At any rate, except for the very poor, benefits were to equal what the individual had paid in, which in the 1930s and 1940s wasn't very much. All that has changed today. Many Americans see their Social Security benefits—which far exceed their contributions—as their entire retirement program. They believe that Social Security is both a substitute for savings and a reason not to save (more on this later).

UNDESIRED EFFECTS

Because of the persuasiveness of the mythology, there is practically universal acceptance by Americans of the Social Security System. People who ordinarily grumble about "welfare queens" driving Cadillacs and who would never accept food stamps accept Social Security payments without a second thought. Moreover, the elderly see Social Security as a right and are quite willing to vote against any honest politician who has the audacity to question either the philosophy or the economics of the system. Acting as a powerful political lobby, they make ending the system impossible and reducing the system's actual benefits practically impossible. As a result, this political lobby of kindly but uninformed elderly people keep pushing Social Security and ultimately the entire economy along the road to disaster. Only a serious reeducational effort can halt this trend.

One of the first educational steps is to see that the Social Security System is really a tax system, and the very worst kind of tax system at that. As presently funded, individuals who are covered by Social Security pay a flat 7.15 percent rate on the first $42,000 of income earned. After $42,000, no taxes are paid. This is a regressive tax, falling more heavily on low-income earners than high-income individuals. The irony is that the low wage earners, who most desperately depend on Social Security, accordingly must pay more out of their current incomes.

Another disadvantage of the method of taxation is that it discourages job creation. With employers required to match the employee's contribution rate, employers find it advantageous to hire fewer workers. This may occur in one of two ways. First, each worker represents a hidden tax payment because employers are required to match employee contributions. By keeping numbers of workers down, taxes and costs are lowered. Second, where employers are already paying the maximum tax because workers are at their maximum wage for paying Social Security contributions, it is desirable to require more work from present workers (and pay more in wages) than to hire new workers and pay the additional employment tax. The macroeconomic effects of such a tax system in reducing employment are obvious, but rarely has a Liberal demand manager come forth to criticize these arrangements.

A second economic fact to be recognized is the unfairness of the benefits. Payments are determined neither by the amount paid in nor by the individual's needs. While some limits to benefits are set according to lifetime contributions to the system, the benefit schedule is connected only loosely to real contribution rates. To a considerable extent, conditions totally unconnected to either need or contributions determine payments to the Social Security recipient. Married persons have greater benefits than the unmarried. A widow who never worked is able to get her late husband's pension. Those who choose to work past the mandated retirement age give up their benefits so long as they work; thus they are penalized for being diligent. Meanwhile, more than 30 percent of all Americans are excluded entirely from Social Security. It is difficult to defend such benefit arrangements. Part insurance in philosophy and part welfare, the benefit program is both unfair to the needy and unequitable to the contributor. Welfare to the truly indigent is perfectly acceptable to a Conservative. Even a system by which a contributor received benefits equal to his or her contribution can be defended logically (so long as the contributions are voluntary). However, we have neither.

An undesirable macroeconomic outcome of the Social Security program has been its impact on savings. As we noted before, the initial object of Social Security was to provide a bare cushion for those who lost their savings in the Depression years. However, as the coverage and benefits of the program—not just old age benefits but everything from educational to health benefits—has grown, Social Security has increasingly been treated as a substitute for personal savings. According to studies by Martin Feldstein, "Social Security depresses personal savings by 30 to 50 percent." The Social Security "contributions" collected by the government are not saved but rather spent on a pay-as-you-go basis. Thus government-forced saving (in withheld contributions) does not replace lost personal savings. The macroeconomic effect of dwindling savings rates is not difficult to estimate. In particular, it denies the nation the fund of savings that would otherwise be available for expanded investment. More consumption and less savings mean less capital. Accordingly, with investment lowered, employment is lowered and unemployment increased. The negative macroeconomic effects of Social Security cannot be overlooked in their impact. Feldstein and others estimate the drag on the GNP to be very great. National output may be reduced by as much as 15 to 20 percent as a result of Social Security discouragement of savings.

WHAT THE NUMBERS TELL US

Despite compelling arguments about the unfair taxing and compensation aspects of Social Security and its drag effect on GNP, the bottom line on the Social Security question is much simpler. It cannot continue to work because (1) there will be too many recipients, (2) benefits are too liberal, and (3) there are too few potential contributors down the road. In other words, it will collapse, not because of any Conservative theoretical criticism, but simply because it cannot pay its own way.

As a result, we face three options: (1) Close down the Social Security System, (2) drastically scale down the benefit structure, or (3) wait for its collapse. Conservatives, naturally, would prefer the first alternative, but recognizing that such a step could at best come only over time, the second scenario seems most likely in the short haul. Quite simply, we must begin to shrink the Social Security System to what it was intended to be—a hedge against personal financial catastrophe and not a guaranteed retirement equal to ordinary living standards. To get individuals to save for their own retirement, the government might legitimately operate its own *voluntary* system of collecting employee contributions (employers should not be forced to pay Social Security benefits or any other retirement contributions unless they choose to do so as an ordinary aspect of wage considerations). Regardless of whether the retirement program is government-operated or carried on by private insurance companies, employee contributions should be seen as savings that grow in value as interest from loaning accumulates. Moreover, an individual's retirement income becomes properly a function of what she or he has decided to save and not a matter of what others think is appropriate. Those unwilling to save for their "golden years" may be paid a very minimum maintenance after they have ceased work, but that is properly a welfare and not a retirement insurance consideration.

Space prohibits extending the present Social Security analogy to the entire welfare system, but it should be obvious from the preceding arguments that what is wrong with Social Security is equally wrong with other components of the social budget. We face a modern-day fiscal crisis of exploding outlays and shrinking ability to pay. The question is not *whether* social outlays will be cut but *how* and *how soon*.

The Liberal Argument

Conservatives are correct when they assert that the Social Security System is the showpiece and the keystone of American social legislation. They are dead wrong, however, when they claim that if this is the case it "proves" the foolishness of government efforts to maintain minimum social welfare conditions. The Conservative allegation with regard to the "bankruptcy" of Social Security financing and their charge that we simply cannot afford the excessive benefits of Social Security are misrepresentations of the facts.

THE IMPORTANCE OF SOCIAL SECURITY

Steeped as it is in the philosophy of voluntaristic and individualistic social behavior, the Conservative argument preaches that it is each person's responsibility to provide for his or her old age or illness. Their arguments, however, fail to point out that this was precisely the kind of social philosophy that prevailed before the New Deal era and before Social Security. Such an individualistic approach to national social welfare was found wanting at that time, and nothing has happened to change the situation. Even in the best of times, the average industrial worker had only the most limited opportunity to set aside a "nest egg" for his or her retirement years. Indeed, most workers in the pre–New Deal era worked until they were physically unable to go on any longer or, more likely, until they were fired by bosses interested in hiring younger, more productive workers. The "declining years" of an elderly worker were often spent in the back bedroom of a son's or daughter's home. This "extended family" condition has received praise lately from Conservative social theorists such as George Gilder, who emphasize the values of family and togetherness. Reality was usually different. Having an old person live with you meant, sooner or later, increased medical bills for the family and almost always long hours of tending the elderly when they became bedridden. Not many who had to go through this sort of thing—neither the old parent nor the children—found life quite so idyllic as modern exponents of the extended family make it seem.

For other poor workers, without savings *and* without family, there was the grim prospect of wasting away in a public institution. "Going to the poorhouse" was not just gallows humor among workers; it was a very real possibility. Usually located on the outskirts of a city, "county homes" and "state homes" had an exquisite institutional ugliness. Workers usually lived dormitory-style; thus husband and wife were separated save for an occasional walk on the premises. The food was of equal quality and quantity to the fare offered at the county jail. There were few social programs for residents to enjoy, just utter boredom until the end.

While Conservatives anguish over the adverse effects of Social Security on private savings habits, their concerns overlook the fact that few American workers were able to save anyway. After Social Security, saving was not only possible but required, as workers and their employers put income aside in trust funds.

For those workers who did succeed in putting away some savings for their later years, the Great Depression of the 1930s demonstrated that there was little virtue in voluntary frugality. As the stock market crashed and banking and financial institutions went under, the elderly of the era watched their savings vanish. Practically overnight, the diligent citizen who had planned ahead for retirement was no better off than the poorest worker or the most profligate. This was the situation when the Social Security Act was passed in 1935. Far from being a destructive "giveaway," it was a very modest attempt to pull millions of elderly Americans out of the terrible insecurity of economic dependency. Conservatives represent Social Security as a step into the collectivist state; the irony is that it returned many elderly people to a condition of economic self-sufficiency and individualism.

As the years passed after 1935, the Social Security System was broadened. First, many additional workers and their dependents came to be covered under the law. Second, the Social Security System was extended to provide health and disability benefits. Third, the payments under Social Security provisions were enlarged. As a result, Americans came to rely on Social Security to handle the economic problems of their retirement years. It became part of a new social contract between government and its citizens, and it is almost universally popular.

It would be wrong to conclude, as Conservatives suggest, that we no longer need Social Security, that the modern-day affluence of Americans would allow a private and voluntary accumulation of savings that would be a "better deal" for workers than the Social Security System. Comparisons with private pension programs are downright misleading. No private insurance company can offer—regardless of the price—a retirement package that includes a pension, health insurance, disability, and life insurance where the benefits are protected from inflation and are also tax-free. Not only is no better plan available, but after a decade of economic contraction, many workers simply could not be certain of meeting their payments for a private program. Thus they would run the risk, as jobs and income decline, of forfeiting their retirement plan. Very quickly, Americans would return to the cruel economic conditions that beset the elderly before 1935.

BALANCING THE BUDGET ON RETIREES' BACKS

The Conservative approach to Social Security is another dimension of their budget-balancing preoccupation, but in this case it misses the point altogether. In fact, Conservatives know full well that their charges of Social Security profligacy and bankruptcy are merely a smoke screen for other objectives. They have been somewhat successful in gaining support for their case because Americans have forgotten the self-funding nature of the Social Security System. Before 1969, Social Security contributions and outlays were not part of a unified federal budget, as they are now. Contributions were paid into trust funds and benefits paid out of these funds. Once contributions and payments were brought into the general budgetary process, Social Security came under new constraints. First of all, the growing outlays for Social Security could now be pointed out as evidence of an expanding welfare state. Never mind that the system was essentially self-funding; no, the growing Social Security expenditures were viewed only as an ordinary budget outlay. Second, after budgetary consolidation, it was possible to think of Social Security benefits as being like any other line item in the budget. In other words, Social Security outlays would be cut just like budgets for national parks or urban development.

Although President Reagan backed off from a number of proposals to trim down Social Security benefits, recognizing as he did the political dynamite in such undertakings, it must be remembered that most Conservatives see the Social Security system as a promising candidate in any effort to reduce federal social outlays.

WE CAN AFFORD IT

The most powerful argument mustered by Conservatives is that the Social Security System is already essentially bankrupt and that in the near future only enormous increases in contribution rates or hefty transfers from general tax revenues will make it possible to continue payments at anywhere near their present levels. If one's focus is only on the old age and survivor's fund, the largest of the system's programs, the Conservative case is, at a superficial level, essentially correct over the next decade. But such a narrow focus obscures the actual condition of the entire system and abruptly closes off the possibilities of long-term reforms that would make the system viable.

First, current difficulties in Social Security funding must be placed in the context of recent economic conditions. For more than a decade, the economy has performed poorly. In the 1970s and early 1980s, prices moved steadily upward, and with Social Security benefits tied to the cost of living, the drain on funds increased. At the same time, wages did not keep pace with prices, and high unemployment held down earnings. Social Security contributions did not keep pace with outgo.

Second, the old age and survivor's fund is only one of the system's programs, and it has not been receiving a large enough share of total contributions. On the other hand, the disability and medical funds have sizable surpluses. The decision in 1984 to allow interfund borrowing was not just a stopgap effort to head off bankruptcy. It was a sound management decision. However, it is true that around 1990 we shall run into a few years when the entire system will be underfunded. This problem could be overcome if the Social Security System was given authority to borrow, just as state unemployment insurance programs presently do. Although such borrowing might never be used, it would at least end the current talk of bankruptcy.

Third, the temporary underfunding will disappear toward the middle of the 1990s as a result of some favorable demographics. The increasingly adverse ratio of recipients (and largely recipients who undercontributed to the fund in their working lifetimes) to contributors will slow down. The post–World War II "baby boom" generation, in the prime of its working life, will be paying into the funds, and a smaller share of the population will be in the retirement category. The buildup should be large enough to produce a surplus in the funds until at least 2020.

Looking at the problem in this way, it is apparent that we *can* afford the Social Security System. By removing it from the unified government budget and by returning to the self-funding system that existed before 1969, the system could be rescued from the politics of the balanced budget and the economics of being traded off against some other social outlay in the federal budget. To further insulate the system from politicians, the system should be removed from its Health and Human Services cabinet department and organized as a separate independent board, perhaps similar to the Federal Reserve System. The point of such efforts is to return Social Security to its earlier nonpartisan place.

Of course, Liberals understand that Social Security is really a "stalking horse" for the entire social welfare structure. Conservatives may be willing to "save" Social Security if other social programs are sacrificed, or they may be willing to accept a trimmed-down Social Security program. The Conservative view rests on the assumption that we, as a people, can no longer pay for the levels of social welfare we accepted as "right and proper" a couple of decades ago. The danger and irony of such an assumption are obvious. The danger is that it accepts abandonment of macro policy efforts to restore growth and virtually accepts the recent downward drift of the economy and the increased maldistribution of income as a fact of economic life. The irony is that even in a shrunken economy, we are asked to find funds for increased military spending (see the previous issue) while sacrificing social outlays. Spending for war is thought to be prudent, but spending for social needs is unwise and wasteful. Such distorted priorities can only threaten the nation's internal political and economic stability.

The Radical Argument

The current crisis in the American Social Security System cannot be understood apart from the general fiscal crisis that grips the government budgets of all modern capitalist economies. From the Radical perspective, we must go beyond the narrow and partisan claims of Liberal and Conservative adversaries and look deeper into the fundamental relations of the state and capitalist enterprise. These real economic relationships, not merely political prejudices, set the actual limits to the growth and development of social spending.

THE STATE BUDGET WITHIN CAPITALIST ECONOMIES

Within a capitalist economic system, the object is always to employ capital and to produce goods in such a way that profits (or surplus over the costs of production) continue to rise. It should be remembered that this is not an arbitrary and doctrinaire definition. Conservatives as well as Liberals know full well that "profits is the name of the game." Conservatives, of course, maintain that government appropriation of the outcome of production (government taxes and their budgetary allocations) come *at the expense* of the private sector. In other words, what government takes and redistributes is a subtraction from what businesses would otherwise receive. Liberals, on the other hand, also see the government taxing and budgetary process as redistributive but defend it on the grounds that either such redistribution is socially desirable or that government spending in fact generates output that would not otherwise take place (see the Liberal argument in Issue 1). Both views, however, miss the important role played by government taxing and budgeting within the modern capitalist state, since they fail to grasp the central place of the state in the process of accumulating capital *and* maintaining social and economic order. In consequence, neither understands the central issues involved in the political and economic struggle over social spending in general or the Social Security System in particular.

If we examine the taxing and budgeting activities of modern capitalist states, it becomes apparent that they pursue two basically different objectives: "accumulation" and "legitimation."* On the one hand, the state undertakes actions that are aimed directly at stimulating economic growth and encouraging business profits (providing for capital accumulation). On the other hand, the state attempts to create and maintain general conditions of social harmony, thus legitimating the operation of a capitalist society. If in fact the state could provide the desired levels of accumulation and legitimation at the same time, there would be no crisis. Nor, of course, would there be much reason to study economics since, in such an Alice in Wonderland world, scarcity would not exist. In the real world, however, these two objectives are competing uses for the state budget. Moreover, as we shall see, outlays for one purpose may be in direct contradiction to the goals of the other objective. The contradiction has become particularly sharp in our era of lagging capitalist growth. Presently, it is obvious that there are very real limits to the budgetary outlays that government can make in these two general areas without (1) raising to unacceptable levels the taxes on the society or on certain groups within the society or (2) generating excessive inflationary pressures (see Issues 2 and 3).

To see how the "accumulation" and "legitimation" functions of the capitalist state budget work, we need only dissect the budget according to these functions. First, there is a broad category of social capital outlays that either *directly* increase capitalist output (social investment) or *indirectly* lower the cost of capitalist production (social

---

*The following analysis adopts the terminology and concepts of James O'Connor, *Fiscal Crisis of the State* (New York: St. Martin's Press, 1973).

consumption). Social investment and social consumption spending add to the accumulation of capital in a variety of ways. Social investment includes outlays for roads, airports, and industrial parks, that is, outlays that increase private-sector output by having government pay for part of the investment cost. Social consumption expenditures such as education and unemployment insurance are useful to business *indirectly*, since the enterprise does not have to pay for training its workers or for sustaining them when economic conditions deteriorate. While social investment and social consumption spending primarily serve the accumulating function, it is obvious that they also work to legitimate the capitalist system. Meanwhile, certain other outlays, which we shall call social expenses, have not the slightest impact on accumulation and work only to achieve legitimation. This is the service performed by those budgetary outlays that commonly are called "welfare"—payments to the surplus or unemployed portion of the population for the purpose of bribing them into complacency and political acceptance of the economic order.

The categories may seem confusing, and in truth the confusion is heightened by the fact that some government outlays serve both accumulation and legitimation ends. Social Security, for instance, lowers the production cost of employers (by having government provide pension funds) and legitimates by sustaining otherwise "useless" workers. Nevertheless, with a little reflection it is possible to categorize government outlays according to how they serve one or both of these basic functions. Such an approach is important because it demystifies the otherwise obscure organization of the government budget. We can begin to see just what certain spending categories are intended to do.

THE GROWING FISCAL CRISIS

Viewing the budget according to the categories of accumulation and legitimation ties together nicely the Radical critique offered in the earlier issues dealing with stabilization policy, unemployment, deficits, and military spending. By looking at how the government budget is constructed according to the conflicting demands of accumulation and legitimation, we can gain insight into the problems of modern macroeconomic policy making. The issue of Social Security becomes understood in the context of a much larger political and economic crisis.

The general fiscal crisis of the modern capitalist state (within which the Social Security crisis is but one small element) can be put simply enough: There are rising demands for government outlays and a dwindling capacity or willingness to pay for such outlays through taxes. Thus the crisis takes a number of forms. First, there is the problem of rising accumulation and legitimation demands. In the current period of economic stagnation, business (in particular the big-business or monopoly sector) requires greater outlays (or what amounts to the same thing, tax cuts) to lower production costs and facilitate capital accumulation. Thus farm subsidies and business "investment credit" programs have continued to expand. Some direct aids to business—such as the "enterprise zone" concept—have been presented inaccurately as if they were really aid to the unemployed worker. Meanwhile, with chronically high unemployment and a stagnation of real income growth, there has been a rise in legitimation claims.

Second, with claims rising, there has been a steady pressure for tax increases. This has stimulated a considerable number of taxpayer revolts such as California's Proposition 13 and dozens of similar efforts to force down taxes. The victory of Ronald Reagan in 1980, perhaps more than anything else, signaled a popular reaction among taxpayers to hold down spending and even to cut it back. Yet when we look at the fiscal restraint actually produced by the tax revolts and by Reagan's victory, we find that few ordinary people have benefited.

The budgetary cuts forced by the fiscal crisis have come primarily from the "legitimation" activities of government. In other words, using Marxist terminology, the budget has become increasingly an instrument of class oppression and domination. Thus budgetary actions that primarily benefit big business and the upper-income groups' abilities to accumulate profits and capital have been protected or have actually expanded, while budget items aimed at maintaining a minimum level of personal well-being have been sacrificed. Quite simply, it is a matter of profits for General Motors and IBM *first*. Conservatives, with their supply-side and trickle-down theories, have been surprisingly honest in putting forth this objective. Even more surprisingly, people who have nothing to gain from such an approach have accepted this nonsense, but only up to a point. Social Security is a good example of how the fiscal crisis can explode into a serious political crisis.

SOCIAL SECURITY AND THE FISCAL CRISIS

The recent shrinkage of purely "legitimation" outlays within the budget, while painful to welfare recipients, never held out much possibility for solving the fiscal crisis. Quite simply, our outlays for the poor always have been too small to provide a significant amount of savings that can be transferred to needed accumulation activities. Moreover, even the wildest-eyed supply-sider knows at heart that literally "starving the poor to death" would bring more political chaos than the system could handle. After all, some minimum outlay must be made for legitimation.

Social Security, with its $200 billion in outlays each year, is certainly a more attractive area from which to obtain accumulation gains. Since "everybody" pays into Social Security and receives its benefits, the class nature of raiding Social Security is not so immediately obvious. If we look beneath the surface, however, we find that the Social Security crisis is an illustrative case showing the basic class nature of government spending and taxing.

On the revenue side, Social Security taxes are collected only on earned income. No taxes are paid from income received from rents, interest, and dividends. Thus the owners of wealth and property are exempted from any payments. Second, the payroll tax itself is regressive, with a constant percentage levied from the first dollar up to a maximum earned-income level. The result is that low-income groups must pay a higher proportion of their income in Social Security taxes. Currently these people are told that Social Security can be saved only by making the tax more regressive, that is, by raising the percentage contribution (and modestly expanding the taxable income level) or by taxing the benefits actually received. This regressive tax structure is encouraged by the fiction that Social Security is self-funding, or that you get according to what you pay in. By keeping the self-funding myth alive, workers are told simply that they can get only what they pay for. If the funds go bankrupt, contributions must increase or benefits must go down. This successfully evades the whole question of guaranteeing minimum retirement benefits irrespective of contributions and allows us to avoid the question of establishing minimum welfare standards for the elderly and the ill. It maintains the capitalist faith that we are responsible only for ourselves and not for others.

Class bias also appears on the benefits side of the Social Security System. Proposals to lengthen the period for retirement eligibility work against the low-income production worker whose ability to work productively is diminished by the physical demands of his or her job. Being forced into early retirement because of health means accepting greatly reduced benefits for the rest of one's life. Meanwhile, well-to-do professionals, who do not suffer from health-damaging employment, are permitted to collect benefits *and* earned income after retirement age has been reached.

The assault on the Social Security System reveals much about capitalism in general and specifically about the current crisis of the capitalist order. First, by attacking Social Security as well as such traditional "legitimation" functions as welfare spending, the defenders of capitalism reveal just how far and how deep the fiscal crisis has developed. The trade-off between accumulation and legitimation activities by the state has become quite severe, a much greater problem certainly than well-meaning Liberal defenders of Social Security understand. Second, both the attack on Social Security and the proposed compromises to save it amount to a new "disciplining" of the working population. Even with its many flaws, Social Security has been an important social welfare program and has been immensely popular with most Americans. Its promise far exceeded its delivery, but it did create a widely held belief that society would indeed protect individuals. Reneging on Social Security sends the signal that this commitment will no longer be honored. Whether Americans are willing to accept this new discipline of reduced social welfare remains to be seen, but the old Liberal program for a system that delivered both accumulation and legitimation is being undone.

ISSUE 7

International Trade and Finance
Free Trade or Protectionism?

> Under a system of a perfectly free commerce, each country naturally devotes its capital and labor to such employments as are most beneficial to each. This pursuit of individual advantage is admirably connected with the universal good of the whole.
>
> *David Ricardo, 1817*

> If nations can learn to provide themselves with full employment by their domestic policy . . . international trade would cease to be what it is, namely, a desperate expedient to maintain employment at home by forcing sales on foreign markets and restricting purchases which if successful will merely shift the problem of unemployment to the neighbor.
>
> *John Maynard Keynes, 1936*

> On the whole, capitalism is growing far more rapidly than before; but this growth is not only becoming more and more uneven in general, its unevenness also manifests itself, in particular, in the decay of countries richest in capital.
>
> *V. I. Lenin, 1916*

> Japanese and German automobile companies have converted Detroit executives from card-carrying free traders to lobbyists for protection to their markets.
>
> *Paul Samuelson, 1980*

THE PROBLEM

Thus far, our survey of contemporary economic issues has centered almost exclusively on purely domestic concerns. The focus is not especially surprising. Until comparatively recently, Americans have not paid much attention to international economic affairs. From the end of World War II to the 1970s, the preeminent position of America in both international trade and finance was pretty much taken for granted by Americans (and by most of the rest of the world too), very much as we took for granted our international political preeminence. Unlike many nations whose very existence depended on foreign trade and commerce, American imports and exports of goods had never been very large, not amounting to much more than 6 percent of our gross national product. As one economist observed of the American tendency to worry little about matters of foreign trade and finance, to do otherwise "would be to let the tail wag the dog."*

Since the early 1970s, however, this attitude of indifference and assuredness has changed. As the Vietnam War was a blow to our international political self-assurance, the oil embargo and the energy crisis of the 1970s and the resulting international economic problems they produced made Americans aware that the world had become a smaller place and that American insularity in international economic affairs was over. Two measures of our changing involvement with the world economy are worth noting.

First, as Figure 7.1 shows, there has been a steady increase in exports and imports as a share of GNP. With growing American investment overseas by multinational corporations and the increasing complexity of multinational production, such a trend was not particularly surprising. It was further accentuated by a growing American dependence on overseas sources of raw materials and, through the 1970s, at least, a growing world dependence on American agricultural products. At any rate, by the early 1980s, foreign trade represented more than 12 percent of the nation's annual output, a doubling of its share of GNP in only ten years. In consequence, America's own economic fortunes became more intimately tied to economic trends and policies at work in other economies, and vice versa.

*Campbell R. McConnell, *Economics: Principles, Problems, and Policies*, 7th ed. (New York: McGraw-Hill, 1977), p. 918.

FIGURE 7.1 EXPORTS AND IMPORTS AS A PERCENT OF GNP, 1929–1985

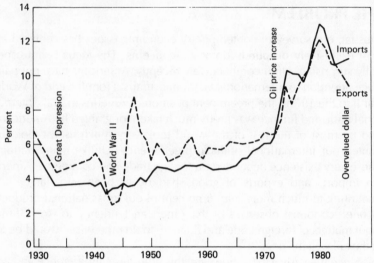

Source: Economic Report of the President, 1985.

Second, and tied to the first development, the United States lost its earlier edge of exports over imports. The overall *balance of international payments* of the United States (the international account measuring all cash inflows and outflows resulting from trade, travel, private capital movement, gifts, and government transactions between the United States and the rest of the world) had been in deficit for some time, but in 1971, for the first time in over eighty years, the nation had a deficit in its merchandise trade balances. Almost uninterrupted thereafter, the United States posted growing trade deficits, as we annually bought more abroad than we sold. Initially, the deficits more or less coincided with the energy crisis of the 1970s. OPEC's actions in levering up oil prices greatly inflated import values. While this generated much immediate concern, presumably an energy independence effort or the eventual collapse of the OPEC cartel would sooner or later solve the problem, or at least so many believed. In fact, the OPEC cartel did fade into comparative insignificance in the early 1980s and world petroleum prices went into a spin, but the United States trade deficit continued to widen. In 1985, the annual deficit was $150 billion. Fully $50 billion dollars of this represented our unfavorable balance of trade with one country, Japan. Also in 1985, the U.S. Department of Commerce reported that the United States had become a "debtor nation" for the first time since 1914, owing more in financial claims to foreigners than the rest of the world owed us.

A variety of factors could be cited for the relative decline of American export capacity and the nation's growing taste for foreign goods. The blame was variously laid to overpriced American labor, poor American management and domestic investment strategies that caused production inefficiences, changing tastes of American consumers, and domestic macroeconomic policies that allegedly first fueled inflation and later produced a bulging federal debt. The latter cause drew considerable attention. There was little denying that the debt and the high-interest money policy chosen to fight domestic inflation made investment in American securities attractive to the rest of the world. This in turn increased foreign demand for U.S. dollars. With such demand high and rising, the dollar strengthened in comparison to other world currencies. This translated into relatively higher prices in world markets for U.S. goods and relatively lower prices for foreign goods in domestic markets. Paradoxically, Americans who had worried about the weak dollar of the 1970s, weakened by raging inflation in the United States, were to find out that a strong dollar could produce the same trade deficits.

Regardless of the causes for the growing trade imbalance, public attitudes fastened in the mid-1980s on the domestic results of buying more abroad while selling relatively less. In particular, the flood of imports was seen as an immediate as well as a long-run threat to American industry and to American jobs. The cure advocated by many politicians, under heavy political pressure to save jobs at home, was to resort to various protectionist proposals—tariffs and import quotas. The old battle between free trade and protectionism surfaced once again, as it had many times before in American history. In the past, Americans had generally shown a preference to protect their markets. Irrespective of whether such a policy was wise, the consequences had been less significant because of America's comparative insularity. In the 1980s, with America more dependent on foreign trade than ever before, the choice of protectionism or free trade had vastly greater consequences to the United States and to the rest of the world.

SYNOPSIS. Conservatives argue that U.S. trade and currency problems are traceable to protectionism, pegged exchange rates, and ill-conceived domestic economic policy. Liberals oppose the Conservative remedy of free trade and floating exchange rates, maintaining that the cost in terms of jobs and industrial decline in the United States would surpass any benefits. They hold that only stimulation of the domestic economy will assure international vitality. To Radicals, the present international trade and finance problems of the United States are a gauge of the nation's decline from power and a further measure of the chronic capitalist crisis of production and distribution.

Anticipating the Arguments

- According to Conservatives, what particular economic problems are caused by protectionism?

- Why do Liberals believe that even worse problems would be caused by free trade and floating exchange rates?

- What do Radicals identify as the cause for recent U.S. balance-of-payments problems?

The Conservative Argument

Perhaps the severest test of commitment to a free and open capitalist economy arises with respect to international trade and finance. Economists, politicians, and especially business leaders who perceive the advantages of competition and the market and who ardently oppose any type of controls or intervention in domestic activities are ever tempted to abandon their philosophy at the national borders. Perhaps it is a narrow nationalism or a basic parochialism in economic thought, but the logic of free markets is too easily abandoned when international issues are raised. For the consistent Conservative, however, there should be no exception in such a case. Free economic arrangements are as crucial internationally as they are domestically.

THE NECESSITY OF FREE TRADE

The first requirement for a free trade arrangement is the elimination of all tariffs, quotas, and bilateral or multilateral trade agreements that inhibit the free operation of international markets. Each nation must be free to sell its goods to any other, and each nation must be open to any other's goods. Regrettably, however, the desire for protectionism runs very deep among nations. This remnant of outmoded mercantilist philosophy persistently reappears when one nation gains a production or price advantage over another in a particular product or line of products. In the United States, it appears when firms or industries act as special-interest groups lobbying Congress to raise duties on hated imports or to set quotas on these imports. Supposedly, by limiting the ability of foreign firms to compete through price or other means, the American industry's position is enhanced.

Ironically (in terms of the long-run effects), labor unions in affected industries very often ally themselves with the corporation in their lobbying effort. For example, in the 1980s, the United Steelworkers joined with the steel industry to urge import restraints on certain "specialty steel" items. From the union's point of view, the object is always to protect jobs. The real outcome is quite different, however, for several reasons.

First, protectionism is costly. It raises the prices of imported goods for all consumers or artificially holds up the price of competing domestic goods. This may mean jobs and income for steelworkers and steel companies in Gary, Indiana, but it means reduced buying power and lost jobs elsewhere. Tariffs and quotas have not protected American earnings but have merely redistributed income and jobs and raised prices for everybody.

Second, protectionism encourages inefficiency. Without the incentive provided by competition, neither business nor labor is induced to increase productivity or to modernize production techniques. In turn, consumers must pay for an industry's protected inefficiency, which can be quite costly over time, since it tends to grow cumulatively. The limits on foreign competition are very often increased as the production gaps between a vibrant overseas producer and a lethargic domestic industry grow.

Third, protectionism invites retaliation. Other nations will be induced to follow the same protectionist path if their goods are effectively priced out of our domestic markets. Thus we may find the threat of foreign steel eliminated at the cost of being unable to sell U.S. tractors in foreign markets. The ultimate result is the end of trade altogether.

Fourth, protectionism invites other undesirable tinkering with trade, exchange rates, and capital flows to effect political solutions to economic problems. For instance, Liberals would attempt artificially to improve our international balance of payments through a variety of interventions. Practically disregarding the favorable effect of inflows of foreign earnings by U.S. businesses on our balance of payments, many Liberals have incorrectly singled out the export of U.S. capital as a primary cause for balance-of-payments deficits. Their shortsighted cure is to restrict U.S. overseas investment. Beginning in 1964, through special taxes on American purchases of foreign securities, overseas investment has been discouraged. As with all protectionist actions, the effect has been counterproductive for the economy. American businesses are placed at a competitive disadvantage in world markets at precisely the time when they should be strengthened.

Free trade and free overseas movement of U.S. capital may indeed mean the end of some American industries and may throw some workers out of jobs. However, other production possibilities are opened. Let the Koreans concentrate on toy or textile production and the United States exploit its computer technology. Indeed, let each nation develop its comparative advantages so that trade between the two is possible.

Milton Friedman has emphasized the significance of a commitment to free trade this way:

> There are few measures we could take that would do more to promote the cause of freedom at home and abroad. Instead of making grants to foreign governments in the name of economic aid—and thereby promoting socialism—while at the same time imposing restrictions on the products they succeed in producing—and thereby hindering free enterprise—we could assume a consistent and principled stance. We could say to the rest of the world: We believe in freedom and intend to practice it. No one can force you to be free. That is your business. But we can offer you full co-operation on equal terms to all. Our market is open to you. Sell here what you can and wish to. Use the proceeds to buy what you wish. In this way co-operation among individuals can be world wide yet free.*

*Milton Friedman, *Capitalism and Freedom* (Chicago: University of Chicago Press, 1962), p. 74.

THE NECESSITY OF FLOATING EXCHANGE RATES

Despite the central importance of free trade policies in developing an efficient and mutually beneficial system of international commerce, free trade alone will not bring freedom to international markets. The other side of the free trade coin is the maintenance of freely floating exchange rates. Indeed, the two must proceed together.

To understand the advantages of flexible exchange rates, we need to see how they work and how pegged rates cause trading difficulties. Take two countries, the United States and Great Britain, for instance. Consider also a particular bundle of representative goods. In Britain, this bundle of goods can presently be purchased for £50, and in the United States an identical bundle costs $100. Accordingly, we can say that £50 buys $100 worth of goods, and vice versa. Thus we can conclude that in terms of a free or floating "exchange," £50 = $100, or £1 = $2 (or, in terms of dollars, $1 = £50). Now consider that inflationary pressures develop in the United States, causing the dollar price of our bundle of goods to rise to $200. If the exchange rates are still floating freely, the new exchange rate will be £1 = $4. Inflation has reduced, both at home and overseas, the buying power of the dollar, which is exactly the effect we would expect of inflation. However, if the United States tried to maintain the old $2 = £1 rate, the official exchange value of dollars to pounds would be overvalued. The price of American goods in Britain would be artificially high. Rather than getting an equivalent bundle of goods for £50, Britons would get only half a bundle for their money if they bought American goods. Meanwhile, in the United States, British goods would be relatively cheaper than American goods. It would take only $2 to buy goods denominated at £1 rather than the $4 that would be required if we had a freely floating exchange rate reflecting the actual 4-to-1 dollars-to-pounds ratio. It becomes immediately obvious that pegged rates that are either above or below the real purchasing power parity (based on our identical bundles of goods) make it impossible for stability to exist in international markets. Nations with currencies that are overvalued relative to those of other nations will actually encourage a worsening balance of trade as import prices are held down and export prices are held up. Meanwhile—and this is a strategy not lost on most nations—undervaluation of a nation's currency tends to encourage exports and discourage imports.

From the end of World War II until the 1970s, the world used a fixed exchange rate system. Under what was known as the Bretton Woods* arrangements, the United States dollar replaced the traditional international unit of account, gold, as the instrument for measuring and making international payments.

To oversee these international transactions, the International Monetary Fund (IMF) was created. The pound, the franc, the mark, the yen, and all other currencies were valued by the IMF against the dollar. Thus when a nation experienced domestic inflation that raised the price of its goods relative to those of other nations, it was obliged, for international money exchange purposes, to devalue its currency in relation to the dollar. If, for instance, the British experienced an inflation that doubled the price (in pounds) of British goods, the only way to bring the inflated British currency into proper balance with unchanged dollars (and other currencies) would be to devalue the pound by one-half. Each dollar would now buy twice as many pounds and twice as much British goods as was possible before the revaluing. If the British did not devalue their currency, trading nations would shun either their products or their currency, and the domestic crisis would be worsened. To forestall short-term shortages of funds for international payments and to avoid the anarchy of devaluation wars as each nation sought to gain a brief currency advantage over others, the trading nations maintained reserve balances with the International Monetary Fund or could borrow from the fund. Meanwhile, the fund pegged currencies to the dollar, adjusting values from time to time as economic conditions within nations changed. So long as the dollar was sound, the problems of inflation or unemployment could be limited to the affected country. The system's weakness, however, was what everyone had thought to be its strength—the dollar.

During the 1950s and 1960s, the previously weakened European and Japanese economies strengthened precisely as the American economy slowed. For the United States, the pegged exchange rate

---

*Meeting at Bretton Woods, New Hampshire, toward the end of World War II, the Allied powers agreed to an "adjustable-peg" system. While exchange rates for individual currencies were pegged to the dollar, their value in dollar terms could be changed to reflect overvaluation or undervaluation.

meant maintaining an overvalued dollar. The result was a growing balance-of-payments deficit during the 1970s as overpriced American goods sold poorly in foreign markets while cheaper foreign goods flooded the United States. Under a pegged system, the only options to eliminate the balance-of-payments deficits were (1) to pay out gold to creditors (so long as we were on an international gold standard), (2) to engineer a domestic recession to lower import demand and reduce the prices of exported goods (thus increasing export volume), (3) to establish import controls, or (4) to resort to an official devaluation of the nation's currency. For a variety of reasons, each of these options has such serious political or economic effects that the balance-of-payments deficit could not be eliminated. As a result, the worsening U.S. payments situation through the early 1970s was directly traceable to the Bretton Woods–IMF system of fixed exchange rates.

Furthermore, the flow of dollars into European markets and the effects of U.S. government efforts to impose exchange controls created extensive internal currency problems for all nations. The initial flood of U.S. dollars and the attempt to maintain the value of these dollars forced an unwanted inflation on many European nations as their central banks purchased all dollars presented to them. With foreigners now holding more dollars than they wanted—dollars that were believed overvalued by the old Bretton Woods pegging system—the United States was forced to take action. On August 15, 1971, President Nixon suspended the dollar's convertibility to gold. At the time, foreign dollar holdings were four times greater than the value of the U.S. gold stock, the price of which was then officially stated as $35 per ounce. Gold henceforth became a speculative commodity having no official role in international payments. It climbed to over $900 per ounce in 1980 before tumbling back to $300–$350 range by the mid-1980s.

After the United States ceased gold conversion, there were periodic efforts to revalue the the dollar under the old pegging system. However, even after several devaluations of the dollar, it became obvious that the era of fixed exchange rates was over. Each nation now let its currency "float" to whatever value the market established, and neither gold nor U.S. dollars served as the international currency. Instead, the IMF kept national payment accounts in order through a kind of "paper gold" (SDRs, special drawing rights), which were made available to members on a quota system. The value of the paper gold is based on an average of five leading nations' currencies.

The drift toward floating exchange rates was a desirable development. If practiced honestly and without the slightest tinkering by governments, floating rates allow nations to trade goods based on their real values as opposed to the manipulated values under pegged rates.

Flexible exchange rates eliminate balance-of-payments deficits and associated problems. The market forces of supply and demand for a nation's currency create an equilibrium. Assume that two nations are trading. An excess of imports over exports in nation A will bid up the price of the currency of the exporting nation B (or lower the value of the importer's currency relative to that of the exporter). Importing nation A's currency is now devalued. However, this means that its goods are now lower-priced than before, and its exports to B will rise while its imports from B will fall until equilibrium between the two trading nations is reached.

From the point of view of most Conservatives, the abandonment of pegged exchange rates and the international gold standard have freed international trade from some of the tyrannies of the past. Gold prices may fluctuate as a matter of speculative supply and demand. In theory at least, floating exchange rates can reflect increasingly the real value of a nation's currency against that of other nations. However, this latter situation has not been attained yet. The present managed float system still allows member nations great latitude in determining their own exchange rates and in taking individual actions to bolster their currency. Until exchange rates are freely flexible and until free trade principles are generally accepted, international trade and currency crises will continue.*

INTERNATIONAL CRISIS AS FAILURE OF DOMESTIC POLICIES

The creation of free trade and freely floating rates, desirable as they are, will not protect a nation that is hell-bent to cut its own

*The argument on behalf of floating exchange rates presented here is the "traditional" Conservative view. It should be noted, however, that some Conservatives, led currently by Robert Mundell, favor a return to the gold standard. This view argues that tying the domestic and international monetary arrangements to a fixed gold standard will create greater stability, making it impossible for nations to export their domestic inflationary policies and to "manipulate" exchange rates to their own advantage.

throat. The recent exchange rate and trading difficulties the United States has faced are the price of an excessively expansionary macro policy that first generated inflation in the 1970s and then brought chronic federal deficits in the 1980s. The price for fighting inflation was high interest rates, which, as we have seen earlier, produced a strong dollar. With the dollar overvalued, an unfavorable trade situation soon developed. It has also produced a growing temptation to return to the bad old days of protective tariffs and pegged exchange rates. The old lie—that trade balances and currency values can be manipulated as desired through public policy efforts—has surfaced again.

The Conservative position is absolutely clear with respect to efforts to set up trade barriers to protect American markets and to manipulate currency values to expand foreign sales: All such interferences with the market mechanism, despite the short-term ill effects of an unfavorable balance of trade, must be opposed if we are ever to obtain the benefits of free international trade. Painful as it may be, we must bite the bullet as the price of our past fiscal and monetary policy excesses.

The Liberal Argument

Typically, Conservatives remain detached from reality and hopelessly utopian in their advocacy of free trade: the *perfect* solution for an *imperfect* world. Although there are, theoretically, greater long-run benefits to be obtained under free trade than under protectionism, Conservatives are calling for America to act as a free trader in a very unfree international economic environment. Playing by Marquess of Queensbury rules while most of the rest of the world cheats has already cost us dearly.

A BACKGROUND TO THE TRADE CRISIS OF THE 1980s

According to the Conservative scenario, free trade and floating exchange rates go hand in hand to produce harmony and equilibrium in international trade and finance. Quite naturally, they oppose any efforts at protection or manipulation of exchange rates. However, they don't seem to make any connection between their own domestic economic policies and the nation's recent trade deficits, prefering to blame it all on past Liberal economic policy.

In point of fact, the incredible decline of American exports and the even more incredible flood of imports after 1980 was the direct result of Conservative domestic policies that had adverse international effects for the United States *precisely because* we had followed a free trade, floating-exchange-rate path. The scenario went like this: The incorrect Conservative view that the late 1970s' inflationary pressures were demand-based (too much spending by government, business, and consumers) led to the adoption of a tight money policy by the Federal Reserve System. Consistent with our macroeconomic understandings, this led to rising real interest rates and eventually to a domestic recession. On the surface, the recession might have been expected to have had a stimulating effect on exports as prices of domestic goods steadied or even fell a bit. However, this did not happen. Instead, in an economic world where exchange rates had become more flexible (after the collapse of the old pegging system), high dollar interest rates in the United States suddenly became attractive to foreign investors. The demand for dollars (to invest in the United States) grew, and as demand grew, the price of the dollar rose. With the dollar now strengthening relative to other currencies, dollar-denominated goods became more expensive in foreign markets while goods denominated in yen, marks, francs, and other currencies became cheaper in the United States. The effect was to depress U.S. exports and invite an explosive increase in imports. The recessed conditions of the domestic economy, stemming as they did from the original tight money policy, were in fact worsened as many key industries were closed out of foreign markets precisely as they were being battered at home by imports.

It suddenly became apparent that domestic economic policies could have unintended international effects in a world of floating exchange rates and free trade. Of course, free traders will argue at this point that sooner or later the overvalued dollar will fall in value as exchange rates adjust. All this supposes, naturally, that exchange rates are in actual fact freely floating, and it presumes that the overvalued dollar will not continue to be propped up by a high-interest-rate money policy.

While it is easy for economic theorists of any political preference to dismiss protectionism as "beggar thy neighbor" economic policy, the recent protectionist sentiment, from a Liberal point of view, is perfectly explainable and not entirely without justification. What we have learned from the trade problems of the 1980s is that pursuit of free trade in a world where few practice free trade and maintenance of floating exchange rates while some nations manage their rates can simply lead to unacceptable economic costs. These costs take the form of destroying certain domestic industries and greatly increasing American unemployment. In short, for all of its theoretical attractiveness, free trade and floating exchange rates can, under some conditions, deliver the opposite of what they promise.

THE CASE FOR MODIFIED PROTECTIONISM

As Figure 7.2 shows, U.S. tariffs have fallen steadily since World War II and stand at historic lows. Duties collected amount to less than 10 percent of the value of imports. Forty-five years ago, du-

FIGURE 7.2   MAJOR U.S. TARIFF AGREEMENTS AND LEVEL OF EFFECTIVE TARIFFS, 1910–1982

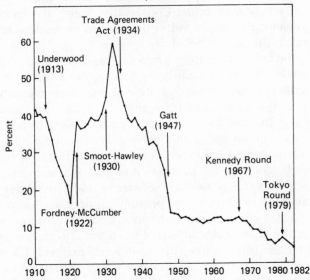

Source: Historical Statistics of the United States and Statistical Abstract of the United States, 1984.

ties stood at about 60 percent. Moreover, the U.S. government has conducted, since the Kennedy years, serious trade negotiations to reduce restrictive tariffs and import quotas throughout the trading world.

But reduction of trade restraints must be a two-way street. Reductions of restrictions on U.S. goods should be expected from nations desiring or obtaining benefits from the United States. Otherwise, the United States throws its doors open to foreign goods while our own goods are effectively excluded from foreign ports. Nor are tariffs and quotas the only devices nations use for creating trade advantages. The Japanese, for instance, have provided extensive governmental subsidies for their manufacturers, thus creating artificially low prices. Their notorious "dumping" of such underpriced commodities as TVs, cameras, specialty steel items, and the like must cease or the United States will be obliged to take restrictive trade actions.

When these real-world obstacles to trade are considered, it is apparent that the road to free trade is much bumpier than Conservatives admit. And apart from the difficulty of inducing all trading nations to accept the principles of free trade (which would be a minimum requirement even under Conservative logic), the serious domestic problems that might follow the hurried or reckless adoption of free trade must be considered.

First, the failure to employ protective tariffs might deal a death blow to many American industries. Among these would be firms that are critical to our capacity to defend ourselves militarily or to our continued economic well-being if world trade were interrupted in the future. In brief, the military and political significance of self-sufficiency in certain goods and raw materials would outweigh the free trade argument of greater efficiency resulting from free trade.

Second, concentrating production efforts only in industrial areas where a nation may have a comparative trade advantage would tend to create an incomplete and possibly unstable economy. As our own production mix became more specialized and concentrated, we would become more vulnerable (not stronger, as Conservatives argue) when there was any interruption in world markets. The serious impact that overseas shortages of critical goods might have domestically has been demonstrated amply by the crises caused by the OPEC energy cartel. Similarly, we might experience interruptions in the purchase of our specialized production when buyers disappeared. The result would be massive layoffs and recession at home.

Third, and closely associated with the first two points, free trade might have the effect of closing off the development of new ("infant") industries. Already established firms would enjoy marketing and capital advantages that could not be overcome. Limited tariff protection would allow new industries to emerge and mature. It is a strategy that has worked well for the Japanese, and we should profit from that lesson since it has been a costly one for the United States.

Fourth, and probably the best-known argument against absolute trade freedom, American firms might be priced out of the market by cheaper foreign labor or by foreign dumping, causing domestic economic upheaval and unemployment. In the short run, free trade, without any quotas or restrictions, would probably produce massive unemployment in basic industries like steel and autos, which would make our current unemployment problems in these industries look inconsequential. Even if, in the long run, new industries emerged to fill the employment gap, billions would be spent on unemployment insurance, welfare, and job retraining. Whole areas of the nation would be disrupted as our nation's production mix changed. Such costs would more than offset the efficiency advantages proposed by Conservatives.

A DIFFERENT VIEW OF EXCHANGE RATES AND PAYMENT IMBALANCES

Although Conservatives are correct in pointing out the foolishness of pegged international exchange rates, whether currencies were tied to gold or to the U.S. dollar, they inaccurately see the present period as a time of largely floating rates. With the exception of the United States, most nations use "managed floating rates." That is, central banks and national governments take actions as they see fit to strengthen or weaken their currency *vis-à-vis* other nations. For instance, by taking actions in the early 1980s to keep the yen undervalued, the Japanese enjoyed selling their commodities in the United States while keeping out the higher-priced (in yen) American goods.

So long as exchange rates are managed—and Conservatives offer no reasonable suggestions for controlling economic nationalism—

free trade will be impossible. Free-trading nations such as the United States have few options except to resort to some forms of protectionism when exchange rates are rigged to open such nations to a flood of imports and to shut off their export markets. The only other option is to manipulate our own exchange rates by taking actions to devalue the dollar (as we in fact did in 1985), to offset other nations' actions. However, in the long run, such action is useless unless other nations consent to our move and do not take offsetting devaluation actions.

The bottom line is that strong international agreements are necessary before freely floating exchange rates and free trade are possible. Ironically, free international trade and finance can be free only if the rules of the game are vigorously enforced. Unless the economic nationalism of states can be brought under control (which implies creating international administrative arrangements that really work rather than depending on some anarchic notion of "freedom"), the benefits of free trade will always be illusory to nations that maintain truly floating exchange rates and open markets.

PUTTING THE INTERNATIONAL ECONOMY IN PERSPECTIVE

Regardless of what happens in terms of developing international "rules of the game" and enforcing them, the United States cannot withdraw from the world economy. On the other hand, we should put it in proper perspective. Probably the most significant problem posed by free trade and floating exchange rates is that the domestic economy is subordinated in international economic affairs. Policies aimed at correcting balance-of-payments and exchange problems may actually worsen domestic problems. For instance, unemployment in the United States would have to grow and an extended domestic recession would be required as the price of ending our international payments deficit.

Free traders may resolve this conflict between needed expansionary policies at home and the required contractionary actions to put our international payments in balance by glibly saying, "We must bite the bullet." Matters are not that simple. Indeed, the contraction might be so unbearable as to trigger extensive political reaction in the United States that would destroy not only our political institutions but even the market economy so beloved by Conservatives.

The real measure of a nation's strength in international affairs is the strength of its domestic economy. Accordingly, the United States may have to undertake limited protectionism and exchange-rate intervention to shield itself. Such actions, of course, must be complemented by domestic microeconomic and macroeconomic policies to stimulate investment and productivity growth; otherwise, the Conservative scenario of a nation decaying behind its own protectionist walls *is* a distinct possibility. However, we shall lose both sight of the real point at issue and any control over it if the seductive logic of free trade leads to a benign neglect of the domestic economy.

The Radical Argument

While the Conservative and Liberal scenarios of international trade and exchange problems seem to be quite different, a closer examination indicates that they are similar. Both arguments accept as a matter of fact the continued domination of the United States in world trade. The remedies that they suggest for current problems, whether it be the free trade approach of the Conservative or the administrative emphasis of the Liberals, are intended primarily to restore and strengthen the American position. Moreover, their underestimation of the significance of international trade and finance and of the degree of crisis now existing in these areas is a dangerous error of judgment.

Capitalist nations do not trade and expand their international influence merely "to improve efficiency" or "to benefit mutually from each nation's exploitation of its comparative advantage." Profit making, pure and simple, is the engine that drives overseas trade and investment. Indeed, the overseas search for markets, cheap resources, and profitable investment is absolutely essential for any capitalist system's continued expansion. Rather than trade and international economic affairs being mere aspects of capitalism, as Conservatives and Liberals suggest, they are the *central features* of modern production-for-profit economies. The international trade and exchange crisis is thus the result of the insatiable drive of individual capitalist nations to exploit the rest of the world for their own gains.

THE RISE OF THE AMERICAN EMPIRE

While Americans tend to think of themselves as reluctant internationalists drawn into world affairs only to save the rest of the world from itself, the facts support quite a different explanation. By the turn of the twentieth century, American capitalism had exhausted its domestic markets. The long decade of depression in the 1890s suggested to many the need for overseas expansion either to obtain markets for our surplus goods or to gain access to cheap raw materials and foreign labor. The United States steadily enlarged its world trade between the 1890s and the 1960s, exporting ever-larger amounts of expensive manufactured goods and importing greater quantities of cheap raw materials. At the same time, to secure markets and assume control over raw materials, Americans exported vast amounts of capital (see Table 7.1).

The old trading powers of Europe exhausted themselves in two world wars, which had been fundamentally economic wars for trade supremacy, while the United States continued to expand its overseas sales, purchases, and investment. By the 1960s, the United States, in terms of comparative development, had reached the peak of its inter-

Table 7.1   Value of Overseas U.S. Investment, Selected Years, 1880–1980 (in billions of dollars)

Year	Amount
1880	1.6
1890	2.9
1900	2.5
1914	3.5
1920	7.0
1930	17.2
1940	12.2
1950	19.0
1960	40.2
1970	75.5
1980	213.5

Source: U.S. Bureau of the Census, *Historical Statistics of the United States* and *Economic Report of the President, 1980.*

national economic power. The rise to this height and the later fall are important and instructive enough to examine in some detail.

In 1950, U.S. gross domestic output was about equal to that of the rest of the world combined. Great Britain's output was only 13 percent of this country's, while those of France, West Germany, and Japan were 10, 8, and 4 percent, respectively. During World War II, the United States, as principal supplier of arms, had accumulated almost the entire world's gold stock, as well as many other overseas assets. Our exports accounted for about one-third of all the world's exports and more than a quarter of all manufactured exports.

Meanwhile, as a result of Marshall Plan aid and other dollar grants to ''free'' European economies, other capitalist nations fell into a simple client relationship with the United States. Dependent economically on aid and trade programs and militarily (in the cold war years) on America's armed forces and mutual defense treaties (such as NATO) that were dominated by the United States, the older capitalist nations became part of the American economic sphere. At the same time, the United States expanded its penetration into the Third World, establishing a new, informal colonial system. Within this imperial system, the resource-rich remnants of the former European colonial empire in Africa and Asia joined Latin America as part of our sphere of influence. Through development aid and especially through the habit of supporting friendly repressive regimes with military assistance, the United States established a neocolonial system that included emerging nations without resorting to the old tactic of territorial seizure.

By the late 1950s, the United States enjoyed a virtually unchallenged economic hegemony over the noncommunist world, comprising the Western European and Japanese economies and much of the Third World. Supposedly, international agencies such as the International Monetary Fund, the World Bank, and the United Nations became arms of American foreign economic and political policy. Under such conditions, it is small wonder that the American dollar became the international medium of exchange and that the international financial situation of the United States appeared so secure. We could virtually dictate exchange rates, and we could hide any balance-of-payments problem by compelling foreign governments to accept and hold dollars rather than demand gold. The ultimate fall from this pinnacle of international power was to be a terrifying experience for Americans.

THE COLLAPSE OF THE EMPIRE

The fall from power was speeded by events overseas and at home. First, the Soviet challenge failed to disappear. The Soviet economy rose swiftly from the ruins of World War II. Despite the Korean War and dozens of other cold war confrontations, the power of cold war ideology in holding the American–Western European alliance together waned as Europeans reevaluated their position within the American empire. This, as much as anything, directed Europe to a more middle-ground approach.

Second, the European economies made their own rapid recoveries in the 1960s. By 1972, the combined gross domestic output of Western Europe and Japan exceeded that of the United States. Accordingly, the U.S. share of world markets declined drastically. Between 1950 and 1972, our share of passenger vehicle production fell from 82 to 29 percent; similarly, steel production fell from 55 to 20 percent and energy production from 50 to 33 percent. At the same time, the other industrial nations began to claim larger shares of the American market. Finished manufactured imports increased almost 300 percent between 1965 and 1970, while U.S. exports of manufactured goods grew by only 80 percent in the same period.

Third, U.S. domination of the Third World declined. Wars of national liberation and the emergence of new regimes committed to an independent political course eroded American influence. The failure of our effort in Vietnam to stem the tide of Third World nationalism only accelerated the decline of the empire. By 1973, the United States was helpless in dealing with the OPEC embargo. In 1979, it could only stand aside quietly as Iran, perhaps one of the most important parts of our earlier neocolonial system, threw out its pro-American government.

Fourth, the emergence of American multinational corporations further weakened the United States. The flight of U.S. capital overseas to the expanding economies in Europe and the Third World accelerated the decline of the U.S. balance-of-payments position. The multinationals' flight left investment and employment gaps at home, with which the nation was ill prepared to deal. By 1971 the

United States registered the first trade imbalance in the century, as imports exceeded exports.

LITTLE HOPE IN SIGHT

Since the early 1970s, the United States' terms of trade with the rest of the world has continued to deteriorate. The energy crisis and domestic inflation in the 1970s first priced American goods out of many foreign markets and eventually brought on a worldwide recession. As the recession ebbed in the early 1980s, the nation found itself locked in serious competition with the European economies and Japan. The old specter of capitalist trade wars, which had already led to two world wars in this century, appeared once again. The United States, now hampered by a strong dollar resulting from domestic efforts to get inflation under control, was beset by continually worsening trade deficits through the mid-1980s. Faced with the loss of foreign markets and the loss of its own domestic markets to growing foreign competition, the nation turned increasingly toward protectionism, that long-discredited policy for protecting profits of domestic industry and for exporting a county's unemployment. Should the American protectionist effort push very far, of course, it would likely be responded to in kind by most of the rest of the world. In turn, as in the 1930s, it could be expected that world trade would dry up and all production-for-profit economies would find sales and profits falling.

From a Radical perspective, the problem has been predictable. The internationalization of capital is only a further step in capitalism's irrational development. The strength of the American overseas economic operations of the 1950s and 1960s was the result of its power to exploit the so-called free world. This country's gains were others' losses. What we saw as a normal situation was an exceptional one. As our capacity to exploit has been challenged by other capitalist economies, by the development of socialist countries, and by Third World independence, our premiere position in world trade and finance has declined. As overseas growth ends, domestic contraction sets in. The specter of another worldwide capitalist depression looms larger. The crisis is, of course, a production crisis—too many goods and too few buyers. It cannot be resolved by dealing purely with money, balance of payments, and exchange rates.

Rather than being the causes of our international economic crisis, our balance-of-payments and exchange problems merely reflect the basic production-distribution problem of the capitalist system. Neither free trade nor protection, and neither floating exchange rates nor pegged rates, offers a long-term solution. Conservative and Liberal solutions are equally irrelevant.

ISSUE 8

National Economic Planning
How Much Planning Do We Want?

In area after area of our national life, we have adopted policies
that unnecessarily threaten the integrity of the individual. . . .
There runs through them the common element: the substitu-
tion of bureaucratic organization and control for market arrangements, the rejection of Adam Smith's great insight.

Milton Friedman, 1970

The premise that under presently existing circumstances, the
country has to husband its resources more carefully, allocate
them more prudently, and match its financial capabilities with
its social priorities would appear to be worth considering.
What many will call state planning would, to the average family, be no more than prudent budgeting.

New York banker, 1974

Whenever the legislature attempts to regulate the differences
between the masters and their workmen, its counsellors are
always the masters.

Adam Smith, 1776

THE PROBLEM

Through the foregoing Conservative, Liberal, and Radical debates on current economic issues, there has been a consistent tension between, on the one hand, the Conservative defense of a free and unregulated economy and, on the other hand, the limited regulation objectives of the Liberals' and the Radicals' general assault on free markets. At issue has been the question of exactly how free or how planned the economy should be. In our closing debate, it is appropriate to deal with this question directly: How much national economic planning do we want?

According to current opinion samplers, national economic planning is highly unpopular with most Americans. In fact, Conservative Republicans were very successful in labeling Liberal Democrats as "centralists" and "social tinkerers" in the elections of 1980 and 1984—successful to the point that they managed to capture the White House twice and gain and maintain control of the Senate. Someone unfamiliar with American history might conclude that this was a ringing and final referendum against any effort to construct even a modestly planned economy. Such a judgment would likely be premature. Popular political belief in the possibilities of national economic planning has frequently surfaced in the past and has been translated into policy. From Alexander Hamilton's efforts laid out in his "Report on Manufacturers" to Henry Clay's American Plan to Woodrow Wilson's progressive New Freedom to Franklin Roosevelt's New Deal, the United States has undergone a number of periods in which varieties of faith in central planning were applied to the nation's economy. Nor are these experiments with central planning mere artifacts of a distant political past.

Less than a decade ago, a Liberal Congress enacted the Humphrey-Hawkins Full Employment and Balanced Growth Act (it passed the Senate by an overwhelming 70–19 margin). The original Humphrey-Hawkins proposal had actually called for the collection of national input and output data on American industry (an essential and first tool in any economic planner's toolbox) and the creation of an Economic Planning Board to set and implement national economic planning objectives. Although these particular proposals narrowly failed inclusion in the final legislation, the Humphrey-Hawkins bill did call for—though obviously without much authority—the coordination of economic policy between the president, Congress, and the Federal Reserve System and the setting of 3 percent adult unemployment as the "official" target for public policy. As Humphrey-Hawkins was debated in 1976–1978, there were those who talked about entering a "new era in American economic affairs" in which governnment played a central role in setting and fulfilling output and employment objectives. Times change quickly, however, and Humphrey-Hawkins has passed out of the memory of most economists and politicians.

As recently as the 1980–1983 recession, even with a staunch defender of free market economics in the White House, another vision of central planning attracted considerable attention, this time with startlingly strong support in the business community. "Industrial policy," as it was known, promised to revitalize American industry through, among other things, the creation of a federal investment bank that would act as a lender of last resort to businesses, especially those "Rustbelt" industries that were particularly hard-pressed. Some Industrial policy advocates urged that the United States develop its own copy of Japan's highly successful MITI (Ministry of International Trade and Industry). MITI had operated since shortly after World War II, directing Japanese industrial development and targeting winners and losers in Japan's export and domestic markets through its control over research and development funds, investment sources, and imports. However, Industrial policy did have its critics in the United States, and it never developed to the point of proposing specific legislation. At any rate, its attractiveness diminished as the recession of the early 1980s lifted.

As this is being written, the mood of the country and the direction of public policy seem to be pushing in the opposite direction from national economic planning. Official policy espouses extensive deregulation of industry and benign neglect of the older tools of policy control. Nevertheless, it should be remembered that economic planning advocacy is largely a cyclical phenomenon. It is reasonably predictable that industrial policy advocates, the advocates of Humphrey-Hawkins objectives, or perhaps even the proponents of more radical and far-reaching economic planning will capture the public's imagination the next time the economy slips into a significant slump. It should also be remembered that national economic planning in one form or another plays a significant, often dominant, role in most of the rest of the world's economies. It would be foolish to assume that a debate over national planning is an irrelevant exercise.

SYNOPSIS. For Conservatives, the adoption of national economic planning would mean the ending of capitalism as a social system and the imposition of an inefficient dictatorship in its place. Liberals, however, see planning as compatible with our mixed capitalist economy, since the essential elements of the system (private property and economic and political freedom) would actually be enhanced by the increased stability planning would provide. To be sure, Liberals advocate only a limited system of planning. Radicals, meanwhile, see present planning proposals only as efforts to maintain the present inequalities and exploitativeness of the capitalist system. To them, planning is essential, but the planning must be done at the level of human needs, not those of the corporation.

Anticipating the Arguments

- What is the Conservatives' fundamental philosophical disagreement with centralized planning efforts?

- How do Liberals argue that planning and a basically capitalistic economic system are compatible?

- What do Radicals mean when they call for planning "for and by people"?

The Conservative Argument

At this stage in our discussion of contemporary economic problems, the Conservative response to the idea of national economic planning should be obvious—or perhaps it would be better to say familiar. National economic planning, in the sense that it means non-market, administrative decisions on output, pricing, employment, capital, and so on, is to be opposed as vigorously as possible. Planning is the final collectivist victory over freedom and individualism. When economic and political authorities, whether they be fascists or communists or even well-meaning Liberals, have the authority to determine all important matters in the economy, there is little else left in life that is beyond their ability to control. *Brave New World* and *Nineteen Eighty-four* are no longer merely science fiction.

The economic criticism of central planning is fairly quickly summarized. First of all, it is profoundly inefficient in terms of theoretical economic principles. Second, empirical evidence on efforts at national economic planning (which is abundant) proves that such planning is ineffective.

NATIONAL PLANNING: THEORETICALLY INEFFICIENT

As we know, under a market system, prices are the signals for economic activity. The decision to produce a particular good can be calculated both in terms of the actual production costs in labor, capital, or resources and in terms of what that particular good costs compared to other goods. As long as the market designates the prices of the factors of production (labor, capital, and resources) and the prices of final goods, we have a rational calculus. As consumers or producers, we can make choices based on a steady and reliable set of indicators. This is not to say that prices will not fluctuate. Of course they will. They are supposed to fluctuate to show changes in demand and supply and thus changes in the cost structure or in consumer satisfaction.

Far from being anarchistic, the market is a planning mechanism. The market works like a system and, as Adam Smith observed in an essay on astronomy written long before his *Wealth of Nations*, ''A system is like a little machine.'' Like a machine, a ''market-planned'' economy has regulators that keep it in balance.

Administrative planning, on the other hand, has no natural internal or external checks on its effectiveness. In an administered economy, levels of output, employment, and the mix of goods are purely matters of political determination. It is not really important whether these goals are set by commissars, Harvard economists, or the duly elected representatives of the people; they are the result of human judgments. They reflect particular individual or collective biases. Not even a computer can tell what output and employment goals are ''correct'' unless it is programmed (by humans) to respond to certain criteria (selected by humans).

Defenders of planning may point out that high levels of growth and employment have been attained in certain planned economies. There is some truth to this, but the argument misses the point. Administrative planning in the Soviet Union during World War II and afterward, and in developing nations more recently, was bound to have some success because of their very primitive level of economic development. When you have nothing and plan something, you can hardly lose, especially if you have authoritarian control over the labor force. It is quite another matter, however, to maintain efficient administrative planning in an advanced and complex economy. (Lately the Soviets have found this out.)

Like market economies, most administered ones use prices to direct economic activity toward predetermined goals. But it should be remembered that these prices, like the goals themselves, are administratively determined. Prices, therefore, do not reflect costs as we speak of them but are merely a rationing technique used to direct labor, capital, output, and, ultimately, social behavior toward certain objectives.

Space prohibits a more detailed theoretical attack on the output and pricing behavior of planned economies, but a brief survey of some of the problems encountered by them may demonstrate the essence of the Conservative critique.

NATIONAL PLANNING: INEFFECTIVE IN PRACTICE

The Soviet Union is a striking example of what can happen when economic mechanisms are subordinated to clearly political objectives. Not unlike the implied long-run objectives of the old Humphrey-Hawkins Act, Soviet goals also include full employment, enforced price stability, and specific production targets for certain goods.

In the Soviet case, full employment means a job for everyone. In an authoritarian collectivist society, this is not a great problem, but there is a big difference between putting people in jobs and having them perform productively. For instance, Soviet plant managers, given output goals by state planners (which must be met or else), may fear a shortage of labor in the future and so "hoard" workers. On other occasions, they may have to hire labor as directed by state authorities, whether or not they need it. In either case, the workers in question will be underemployed. In terms of economic analysis, the result is obvious. Workers are hired without any view to their productivity. Wages are set by state planners, who have little or no knowledge of costs of production at a plant. Thus managers may reach their output targets, with workers "fully employed," but the actual cost of goods (as reckoned by alternative uses of labor and capital) may be much higher than the planners can cover in setting a price. In real terms this means that the whole society must pay the actual costs by forgoing other goods. An inefficiently made tractor may "cost" many thousands of nonproduced consumer items.

The tendency to think only in output (quantitative) terms has qualitative effects, too. Production rushed to meet a planner's goal may encourage defective and shoddy manufacture. Quick and flexible adaptation of production to meet changes in goals is very difficult. Planners lack the signals of prices based on supply and demand to tell them when and how to change the production mix. Plans become rigid, at both the plant and planning levels.

Many of the worst features of central planning have been improved in the past decade or so by the introduction of linear programming, input-output analysis, and computers. The incredible lapses of mind that led to production of motor vehicles but not the needed ball bearings for their wheels are now rather rare. In many respects, Soviet industry and technology are very advanced. Nevertheless, microeconomic decision making is still hampered by the political administration of prices, wages, and output goals. After years of sacrifice to build the industrial base of the society, ordinary Soviet citizens remain as they always have been, the balancing item in the central plan ledger. The errors of planners, even those with computers, are paid for in relinquished consumer goods and a scarcely improving standard of living. Overarching all of this, of course, is the virtual absence of individual freedom, economic or political.

A LAST WORD

All of this argument may be considered an overreaction to the comparatively innocuous Humphrey-Hawkins Act or to other recent appeals for industrial planning (even by business groups). To Conservatives, though, the threat of planning is quite real. Talk of national economic planning goes back a long way in American history, and, as is evident in day-to-day government reaction to the issues discussed in this book, the tendency toward collectivist solutions to all economic problems, although diminishing a bit lately, remains strong. History shows that, once commenced, the march toward collectivism is hard to reverse. Today we may be talking merely of obtaining additional data for national planning or making "full employment" a law. Tomorrow, the managed-economy objectives may be more personal to all of us—where we live, where we work, what we buy, and so on.

Conservatives are not anarchists. Indeed, they believe in planning, and today we have a high order of acceptable planning in the economy. This planning, however, is a function of individual choices collectively expressed in the market. As Milton Friedman has observed:

> Fundamentally, there are only two ways of coordinating the economic activities of millions. One is central direction involving the use of coercion—the technique of the army and of the modern totalitarian state. The other is voluntary cooperation of individuals—the technique of the market place. . . . Exchange can bring about coordination without coercion.*

The present in-between, never-never land of mixed American capitalism cannot continue long. *We must go either one way or the other in the future.*

The Liberal Argument

The public furor created by discussions of planning arises out of ignorance. Planning as envisioned in the original Humphrey-Hawkins proposal, irrespective of our recent policy turn toward deregulation and "minimum government," was not a sharp divergence from the past. It was basically an elaboration of the principles laid out, but not specifically implemented, in the Employment Act of 1946. Nor is planning in general at all new to the American economy. After all, the government budget is not constructed without calculating the impact of its spending and taxing, nor does Exxon make annual profits of more than $4 billion accidentally. Regrettably, planning calls up the image of a Soviet-type society when in fact it is essential for the improvement of our own democratic capitalism. The type of planning being given serious consideration at present is not an Orwellian nightmare where "Big Brother is watching you." Aside from creating jobs and improving efficiency, it is not intended to al-

---

*Milton Friedman, *Capitalism and Freedom* (Chicago: University of Chicago Press, 1962), p. 13.

ter American life very much at all. In fact, planning is intended to protect, as much as possible, the conditions to which we have become accustomed.

IN DEFENSE OF PLANNING

At this point in our discussions, the Liberal defense of planning need not be lengthy. The necessity for some type of general control mechanism has been evident in all our comments on contemporary policy issues. A shift toward self-conscious national planning, however, would be a major effort to integrate the separate planning and control efforts on which we now depend.

The need for an integrated governmental planning operation will be accepted sooner or later. The crises of energy, employment, inflation, and public finance cannot be dealt with continually in ad hoc policy making. The multiplication and lack of integration of these separate efforts are wasteful and counterproductive. For instance, an energy conservation policy constructed without specific commitment to employment and price objectives may save us fuel but cost us jobs and investment. The great virtue of national planning efforts is that they recognize the interconnection of all economic problems and hence seek solutions in a broad rather than narrow way.

Collection of adequate production data will make it possible to target general objectives in the economy—say, a certain acceptable level of economic growth in particular industries. Balance can be created among industries, such as that needed between developing public transportation on the one hand and sustaining the private automobile industry on the other.

As a rule, coercion will not be necessary to assure that targets are attained. Careful use of tax-subsidy incentives and participation by capital and labor in the planning process can generate a high order of consensus among the constituent parts of the economy. Meanwhile, with government acting positively as a guarantor of jobs in the last resort, the persistent unemployment problem can be laid to rest.

Of course, we must expect crises from time to time, and mere targets or gentle nudging will not always be enough. War, oil embargoes, and international economic difficulties beyond our control may necessitate some coercive use of planning. Such situations may demand rationing of goods, rigorous wage and price controls, perhaps more. However, in the face of serious crisis, the nation would have no other alternative—any more than it had an alternative to rationing and controls during World War II.

Conservative defenders of the market philosophy invariably argue that planning always fails. Usually they dredge up the Soviet Union as the classic planning failure, or they turn to past, ill-conceived American efforts such as Richard Nixon's attempts in the 1970s to maintain wage and price controls. And then there is China—once a rigidly planned and controlled economy, now shifting toward experimentation with market capitalism. However, Conservatives neatly avoid the planning successes. The inherent failure of planning will come as a considerable surprise to the French, the Germans, the Scandinavians, and the Japanese, all of whom have relied on some forms of planning to produce economic miracles over the past three decades. Indeed, the Japanese case has been particularly instructive to American business leaders, who are increasingly aware that Japan's industrial policy of subsidizing and directing key segments of its economy has made the Japanese economy more dynamic than our own. Many have recently begun advocating adaptation of certain elements of Japanese planning for the American economy.

As two Liberal defenders of planning, Robert Heilbroner and Lester Thurow, have observed:

> Planning may well be to our era what the discovery of the Keynesian explanation of depression was to the era of the 1930s. Keynesian policies did not solve the economic difficulties of that era by any matter of means, but they did get us through a period that threatened to plunge us into very serious social and political trouble. Perhaps the proper estimate of planning is much the same. We should not realistically hope that it will solve many of the problems that beset our times—problems of technology, of bureaucracy, of a terrible division of the world between rich and poor—but planning may nevertheless get us through this period of drift and disappointment. That would be quite enough.*

---

*Robert Heilbroner and Lester Thurow, *The Economic Problem Newsletter* (Englewood Cliffs, N.J.: Prentice-Hall, Spring 1976), p. 3.

The Liberal who is challenged to defend planning in principle and practice has only one answer: "Given where we are, is there any other way?"

PLANNING AND CAPITALISM

We cannot leave this topic without taking up the Conservative charge that planning means the end of capitalism. If by capitalism the Conservatives mean the quaint little world of Adam Smith where everyone higgled and sold freely and equally, that world passed out of existence a very long time ago—if in fact it ever existed. The tragicomic Conservative defenders of individualism and freedom have failed to adapt these values to a highly complex technological world. The mutual economic interdependence of people, nations, and institutions simply does not allow us to talk of freedom in such a simplistic sense. The freedom to be poor, the freedom to starve, or the freedom to collapse into social anarchy is really the long-run outcome of efforts to return to a marketplace mentality.

Contrary to the Conservative outlook, planning is not necessarily communism, nor is it authoritarianism of any special breed. Planning is essential to maintaining the American democratic capitalist tradition. To the Liberal, of course, "democratic" is much more important than "capitalist" in a generic sense. The economic experience of the United States and all other basically "capitalist" countries indicates quite clearly that only planning can save the private-property, production-for-profit system from self-destruction. The perquisites of capitalist production, however, must be limited and subordinated to general social objectives. The only apparatus to protect the general society is the state, and the only means open to the state is planning.

While he has not always been in the mainstream of Liberal opinion, John Kenneth Galbraith's observations of two decades ago fairly represent the Liberal position today. After weighing the growing problems of American industrial society, Galbraith concluded:

> It is through the state that the society must assert the superior claim of aesthetic over economic goals and particularly of environment over cost. It is to the state we must look for freedom of individual choice as

to toil. . . . If the state is to serve these ends, the scientific and educational estate and larger intellectual community must be aware of their power and their opportunity and they must use them. There is no one else.*

The Radical Argument

Despite the current Conservative celebration of a renaissance of "free market" thought and practice, capitalism has for a considerable period of time moved inexorably toward greater central control. Although there is considerable debate as to how close we really are to a formally planned and controlled economy, Radicals would generally agree that it is the next great leap in capitalist development. From laissez-faire to monopoly capitalism to state-corporate regulation to formal planning—capitalism runs its course in its effort to secure profit and protect itself. The obvious irony, of course, is that planned capitalism is a contradiction in terms. As the basic economics textbooks tell us, capitalism emerged as a totally free economic philosophy. It ends as a totally authoritarian one.

CAPITALISM NEEDS PLANNING

Ideologies, even after they have proved worthless, die hard, often convulsively. It remains to be seen how the outmoded rhetoric of laissez-faire or even the more sophisticated mixed-economy philosophies will pass into history. They are deeply rooted in the individual practice and thought of American citizens, and their public defenders are still loud and shrill. Nevertheless, as our discussions of other contemporary issues should indicate, the use of government intervention in the economy is apparent everywhere.

This process is not really very new. It originated in the late nineteenth-century response to the growing crises of American capitalism. Troubled by periodic panics or recessions (in 1873, 1885, 1893, and 1907), chronic excess capacity and overproduction, and anarchic market conditions, and threatened by increasingly radicalized labor strife, American capitalism depended more and more on state intervention. We have elaborated on these interventions in our dis-

*John K. Galbraith, *The New Industrial State* (Boston: Houghton Mifflin, 1967), p. 335.

cussions of stabilization policy, government deficits, unemployment, and international trade. As the state became a partner in supporting business, American corporations enlarged their monopoly powers through concentration and control.

This growth of state-corporate integration has been euphemistically termed the "mixed economy" in economics texts. Uninformed Conservatives attacked this integration as the domination of business by the state, without even stopping to ask just whose interests the state represented. They fail to see that, quite as Marx specified, "the State is the form in which the individuals of the ruling class assert their common interests."

Capitalist production has proved to be extraordinarily rational in a microeconomic sense. The organization of production, labor, and capital for any particular firm is governed by economic rules of behavior (we would call it the price system), which, for an individual entrepreneur, give key signals as to how best to attain profit objectives. Yet in totality, the capitalist system is irrational. Though the actions of any given firm are rationally "planned" or calculated with profit in mind, the actions of all firms taken together produce macroeconomic and social disorder. There is a lack of coordination and integration, even among monopolistic capitalists, in dealing with different industries and different sectors of the economy. Rational control of the whole labor force, of total output, and of investment alternatives is lacking.

The boom-bust rhythm of the business cycle, although recently muted when compared to the past, is still evident—but with a difference. Today's highly integrated and automated production is extremely vulnerable to even the slightest variations in sales, profits, and output. In the past, when industry was predominantly labor-intensive, a business downturn amounted mainly to sending the workers home with empty pay envelopes and waiting until things got better. Today, with greater capital usage and production on an international scale, nonproduction presents a firm with greater losses. These, in turn, affect financial markets and the international structure of business.

Moreover, modern capitalism has so penetrated the world that it is limited in its ability to acquire new markets, so essential to its survival. At the same time, as we have noted repeatedly before, capitalist production can be carried on at higher output levels using less labor power. As a result, the crowning irrationality of the system is that it can produce more and more, but labor becomes increasingly redundant and markets harder to find.

The chronic tendency toward unemployment and excess capacity, the steady threat of inflation, and the worsening balance-of-trade situation leave few options for American capitalism. As the Liberal John Kenneth Galbraith has argued for years, the next step in capitalist development is to transcend the market and modern Keynesian efforts to correct it and to move straight toward direct economic planning and controls. Only through such efforts can capitalist irrationality be controlled. Planning presents possibilities for reorganizing the capitalist processes of production and accumulation and at the same time can "legitimize" or bring order to labor markets. The importance of this function of legitimizing was not overlooked in the Humphrey-Hawkins Act, which called for government to maintain full employment (that is, no more than 3 percent unemployed among adults).

PLANNING FOR PROFITS, NOT PEOPLE

The name of the game in capitalism is profits, and the name does not change when capitalist systems adopt centralist planning techniques. Two examples are worth noting.

The Liberal effort at central planning for full employment in the Humphrey-Hawkins debates in the mid-1970s (and there is little reason to believe that die-hard Liberals have changed their positions much) called for specific government planning actions. First, government output "recommendations" were to act as a general guide to business in undertaking specific investment and output decisions. This "indicative" planning can show beforehand where shortages and bottlenecks might appear; it presupposes that rational capitalists will take actions to eliminate such problems. The second aspect of this planning would be selective tax cutting to induce business to move toward certain production goals. This "tax-cutting planning" is really only a dressed-up version of modern Keynesianism. Accordingly, it has, built in, all of the problems associated with trying to generate employment increases by pumping up aggregate demand (see Issues 1, 2, and 3). As we have seen, this may produce short-run profits, but it also generates longer-run cost pressures.

Sooner or later, in the form of inflationary real-wage reductions or perhaps imposed wage controls, workers end up paying for the profits with lowered real wages. If the planning is extensive enough, it may in fact put millions back to work, but only by lowering the real living standards of American workers. The classical economic doctrine of the "iron law of wages" (that incomes should equal subsistence) would be reintroduced through tax transfers and wage controls.

A more blatant profits-first approach to planning, attractive to some Liberals and even a few Conservatives, has surfaced in the so-called industrial policy debate. The inspiration that has attracted a number of business leaders to endorse joint government-business coordination of investment, labor policy, and trade policy to "halt the deindustrialization of America" is pure greed. Presumably, an effective industrial policy would determine winners and losers among American enterprises (since surely not everyone can be a winner), very much as the Japanese have done over the past twenty or thirty years. Industrial policy is obviously popular with present losers, those whose profits have fallen in the perpetual capitalist game of survival. Industrial policy promises improved profits for the losers by either insulating them from competition (thus raising their sales) or lowering their investment and even their labor costs.

In the short run, industrial policy efforts could indeed raise profits, but without much or any gain for ordinary workers or consumers. Goods prices would have to rise if tariffs or quotas were used to protect certain threatened industries. Increased government investment subsidies, as noted earlier, must sooner or later be translated into losses of consumer buying power either via inflation or through tax increases. In all of this, labor will be expected to be disciplined, like Japanese labor, making the sacrifices in both wages and intensified work requirements necessary for keeping costs down and profits up. Recognizing this, some industrial policy proponents have advocated that organized labor be included in the general planning procedures. While the participation of labor in the planning process has certain obvious attractions from a Radical point of view, it is necessary to recognize that most such proposals to date have included labor only as window dressing.

In both of the planning scenarios cited, profits are the central concern, and if profits are to be maintained at all, they are main-

tained at the cost of real losses for workers. Under such planning arrangements, the basic antagonisms and contradictions of capitalism
are not eliminated. They now become embedded in the institutional
apparatus of national economic planning. Planning for people's
needs simply does not take place.

THE RADICAL ALTERNATIVE: PLANNING *FOR* AND *BY* PEOPLE

Although Radicals may be divided on the means by which social
planning is to be achieved—some seeing class revolution as the tool
and others willing to work within the framework of traditional
American political institutions—there is greater agreement on *how*
such planning should proceed once it is established. First of all, most
American Radicals would reject out of hand the varieties of social
planning demonstrated by such socialist nations as the Soviet Union
or Cuba. These efforts at "state planning" have lost sight of the major objective of any rational and humane planning effort: *people*. In
these cases, plans have been developed and imposed from above by
central planning or political authorities whose decisions have no
more to do with workers' and consumers' needs than decisions currently made by Exxon or IBM officials.

The first and unifying rule for Radicals with regard to planning
is that the planning process must begin with popular participation
and must be conceived to deal with "people's problems." There are
of course many levels of planning, from decisions that are made per-
taining to a particular plant or factory to broad national output targets. Obviously, the more distant the level of planning, the more difficult individual participation becomes. However, it does not become
impossible. Recognizing that the Soviet and Cuban cases are examples of what can happen when planning becomes too abstracted
from popular input, the object is always to keep as much of the decision making at the lower levels as possible and, when that is no
longer a reasonable alternative, to devise the broader elements of the
plan through as democratic means as possible.

Workers or their directly elected representatives must be the basis for local output, pricing, and workplace decisions. Such decisions, of course, must be made with an eye to the general welfare.
No worker or group of workers has the right to earnings obtained by

sacrificing consumers or some other group of workers. That would merely be capitalism reappearing in the disguise of socialism, and it would lead to precisely the same kind of exploitative conditions we now live under. Thus it is obvious that workers must be joined by consumers in the local or lower-level planning activities. Organizing broad popular participation in the planning process will not be easy, nor is there absolute certainty that a democratically devised plan will not be guilty of error and even failure. It is comparatively easy for Conservatives and Liberals to paint a picture of chaotic planning meetings as various representatives of workers, managers, and consumers determine key economic objectives. However, they miss three very important points. First, the "failures" of such planning efforts can be little worse than the current private planning "successes." Second, even at its worst, planning based on workers' and consumers' participation *is* democratic planning and *is* consistent with the professed ideals of a democratic society. Third, there are examples of successful participatory planning by workers. Yugoslavia, a maverick Marxist state that is not well endowed with natural resources, has prospered for decades under a decentralized and democratic planning program very much like the general Radical program described here.

Regardless of the precise methods ultimately devised to facilitate participatory planning—and trial and error will certainly play a role in selecting planning goals—the Radical holds to a basically simple belief that the people must be the architects of their own society. The basic economic decisions of what is produced, how, and for whom must not be entrusted to an elite, whether they be capitalists or political commissars.

The Radical economic and social historian William Appleman Williams put it this way:

> Hence the issue is not whether to decentralize the economy and politics of the country, but rather how to do so. . . . This literal reconstructing and rebuilding of American society offers the only physical and intellectual challenge capable of absorbing and giving focus to the physical and intellectual resources of the country during the next generation. . . .
>
> Throughout such a process, moreover, the participants will be educating themselves . . . for their membership in the truly human community they will be creating. In the end they will have built a physical

America which will be beautiful instead of ugly, and which will facilitate human relationships instead of dividing men into separate functional elements. They will have evolved a political system which is democratic in form and social in content. And they will be prepared . . . to function as men and women who can define their own identity, and their relationships with each other, outside the confining limits of property and the bruising and destructive dynamics of the competitive marketplace. They will be ready to explore the frontier of their own humanity.*

*William A. Williams, *The Great Evasion* (Chicago: Quadrangle Books, 1964), pp. 175–176.

PART 3

CONCLUSION

Final Thoughts and Suggested Readings

Having reached the end of this volume of debates on contemporary economic issues, it is probable that the reader expects (perhaps even hopes for) the author to make his own pitch—to say straight out which of the representative paradigms is correct and which is not, perhaps to unveil his own grand program. Indeed, the opportunity is tempting. For an economist, it is practically a reflex to try to get in the last word, especially one's own last word. However, after much thought, I decided that such a conclusion would spoil the entire effort. The book was undertaken to present the differing ideological alternatives as objectively as space and writing talents allowed so that the reader would be free to make personal choices on matters of economic policy.

I can hear some readers complaining: "Cop-out! You're avoiding presenting your own preferences and your own conclusions. You've taken the easy way out of the swamp." Not so. Delivering my own final polemic would in truth be ever so easy. But the book has been about questions and choices. The reader, then, shall be left in the uncomfortable position of making a choice among the paradigms and policy questions surveyed here. And that is the way it should be.

This perspective, however, must not be misunderstood. The author has not intended to produce a "relativistic" conclusion in which any choice will do and one choice is as good as any other. The point is for the reader to make a *good* choice, and some policy choices *are* better than others. However, only a reasoned analysis of the facts and a critical study of the "truths" of this world will permit any of us to make wise choices.

The British economist Joan Robinson has said it best:

> Social life will always present mankind with a choice of evils. No metaphysical solution that can ever be formulated will seem satisfactory for long. The solutions offered by economists were no less delusory than those of the theologians that they displaced.
>
> All the same we must not abandon the hope that economics can make an advance towards science, or the faith that enlightenment is not useless. It is necessary to clear the decaying remnants of obsolete metaphysics out of the way before we can go forward.
>
> The first essential for economists, arguing amongst themselves, is to "try very seriously," as Professor Popper says that natural scientists do, "to avoid talking at cross purposes."*

Before we can "avoid talking at cross purposes" on economic matters, we must understand our fundamental differences in opinion and interpretation. Hopefully, this book has identified some of these important differences for the reader.

In undertaking this task, any author would be sorely tested. While trying to submerge personal biases, one also must master the biases of others. Perhaps I have not entirely succeeded on either count. Only the reader can judge. Nevertheless, such an undertaking is extremely educational. It compels one to work through unfamiliar logic and ideas and weigh them against one's own beliefs. For readers who desire to dig deeper into economic ideologies and their application to contemporary issues, the following bibliography offers some landmark readings in the respective Conservative, Liberal, and Radical schools of economic thought.

---

*Joan Robinson, *Economic Philosophy* (Garden City, N.Y.: Anchor Books, 1964), pp. 147–148.

Conservative

Banfield, Edward C. *The Unheavenly City*. Boston: Little, Brown, 1970.

Buckley, William. *Up from Liberalism*. New York: Honor Books, 1959.

Friedman, Milton. *Capitalism and Freedom*. Chicago: University of Chicago Press, 1962.

_____. *Free to Choose*. New York: Harcourt Brace Jovanovich, 1980.

Gilder, George. *Wealth and Power*. New York: Basic Books, 1981.

Hazlitt, Henry. *The Failure of the ''New Economics'': An Analysis of the Keynesian Fallacies*. New York: Van Nostrand, 1959.

Kirk, Russell. *The Conservative Mind*. Chicago: Regnery, 1954.

Klamer, Arjo. *Conversations with Economists*. Totowa, N.J.: Rowman & Allanhold, 1983.

Knight, Frank. *Freedom and Reform*. New York: Harper & Row, 1947.

Rand, Ayn. *Capitalism: The Unknown Ideal*. New York: New American Library Signet Books, 1967.

Simon, William E. *A Time for Action*. New York: Berkley, 1980.

Simons, Henry C. *A Positive Program for Laissez-Faire*. Chicago: University of Chicago Press, 1934.

Smith, Adam. *An Inquiry into the Nature and Causes of the Wealth of Nations*, 1776.

Stein, Herbert. *Presidential Economics: The Making of Economic Policy from Roosevelt to Reagan and Beyond*. New York: Simon and Schuster, 1985.

Von Hayek, Friedrich. *The Road to Serfdom*. Chicago: University of Chicago Press, 1944.

Von Mises, Ludwig. *Socialism: An Economic and Sociological Analysis*. New Haven, Conn.: Yale University Press, 1959.

Liberal

Berle, Adolf A. *The Twentieth Century Capitalist Revolution*. New York: Harcourt Brace Jovanovich, 1954.

Clark, John M. *Alternative to Serfdom*. New York: Random House/Vintage Books, 1960.

_____. *Social Control of Business*. New York: McGraw-Hill, 1939.

Galbraith, John Kenneth. *The Affluent Society*. Boston: Houghton Mifflin, 1971.

_____. *Economics and the Public Purpose*. Boston. Houghton Mifflin, 1973.

_____. *The New Industrial State*. Boston: Houghton Mifflin, 1967.

Hansen, Alvin. *The American Economy*. New York: McGraw-Hill, 1957.

Heilbroner, Robert. "The Future of Capitalism," in *The Limits of American Capitalism*. New York: Harper & Row, 1966.

Heller, Walter W. *The Economy: Old Myths and New Realities*. New York: Norton, 1976.

Keynes, John M. *The General Theory of Employment, Interest, and Money*. New York: Harcourt Brace Jovanovich, 1936.

Lekachman, Robert. *The Age of Keynes*. New York: Random House, 1966.

Okun, Arthur M. *The Political Economy of Prosperity*. New York: Norton, 1970.

Reagan, Michael D. *The Managed Economy*. New York: Oxford University Press, 1963.

Shonfield, Andres. *Modern Capitalism: The Changing Balance of Public and Private Power*. New York: Oxford University Press, 1965.

Thurow, Lester C. *Dangerous Currents*. New York: Random House, 1983.

———. *The Zero-Sum Society*. New York: Basic Books, 1980.

Radical

Baran, Paul. *The Political Economy of Growth*. New York: Monthly Review Press, 1957.

———, and Paul M. Sweezy. *Monopoly Capital*. New York: Monthly Review Press, 1966.

Bowles, Samuel, and Herbert Gintis. *Property, Community, and the Contradictions of Modern Social Thought*. New York: Basic Books, 1986.

Domhoff, William. *Who Rules America?* Englewood Cliffs, N.J.: Prentice-Hall, 1967.

Dowd, Douglas. *The Twisted Dream*. Cambridge, Mass.: Winthrop, 1974.

Franklin, Raymond S. *American Capitalism: Two Visions*. New York: Random House, 1977.

Kolko, Gabriel. *Wealth and Power in America*. New York: Praeger, 1962.

Magdoff, Harry. *The Age of Imperialism*. New York: Monthly Review Press, 1967.

Mandel, Ernest. *Marxist Economic Theory*. New York: Monthly Review Press, 1967.

Marx, Karl. *Capital*. 1867.

O'Connor, James. *The Fiscal Crisis of the State*. New York: St. Martin's Press, 1973.

Robinson, Joan. *An Essay on Marxian Economics*. London: Macmillan, 1942.

Sherman, Howard. *Radical Political Economy*. New York: Basic Books, 1972.

———. *Stagflation: A Radical Theory of Unemployment and Inflation*. New York: Harper & Row, 1976.

Strachey, John. *The Nature of Capitalist Crisis*. New York: Covici, Friede, 1933.

_____. *The Theory and Practice of Socialism*. New York: Random House, 1936.

Sweezy, Paul. *The Theory of Capitalist Development*. New York: Monthly Review Press, 1942.

Williams, William A. *The Great Evasion*. Chicago: Quadrangle Books, 1964.

Index